This book is due on the last date stamped below.
Failure to return books on the date due may result
in assessment of overdue fees.

Sacramento, CA 95841

USA TODAY'S DEBATE: VOICES AND PERSPECTIVES

GUN CONTROL

Preventing Violence or Crushing Constitutional Rights?

Matt Doeden

Twenty-First Century Books
A division of Lerner Publishing Group, Inc.
241 First Avenue North
Minneapolis, MN 55401 U.S.A.

Website address: www.lernerbooks.com

Library of Congress Cataloging-in-Publication Data

Doeden, Matt.
    Gun control : preventing violence or crushing constitutional rights? / by Matt Doeden.
        p.   cm. — (USA Today's debate—voices and perspectives)
    Includes bibliographical references and index.
    ISBN 978–0–7613–6433–7 (lib. bdg. : alk. paper)
    1. Gun control—United States—Juvenile literature. 2. Firearms ownership—United States—Juvenile literature. 3. Firearms—Law and legislation—United States—Juvenile literature. I. Title.
    HV7436.D64 2012
    363.330973—dc22   2010051919

Manufactured in the United States of America
1 – MG – 7-15-11

CONTENTS

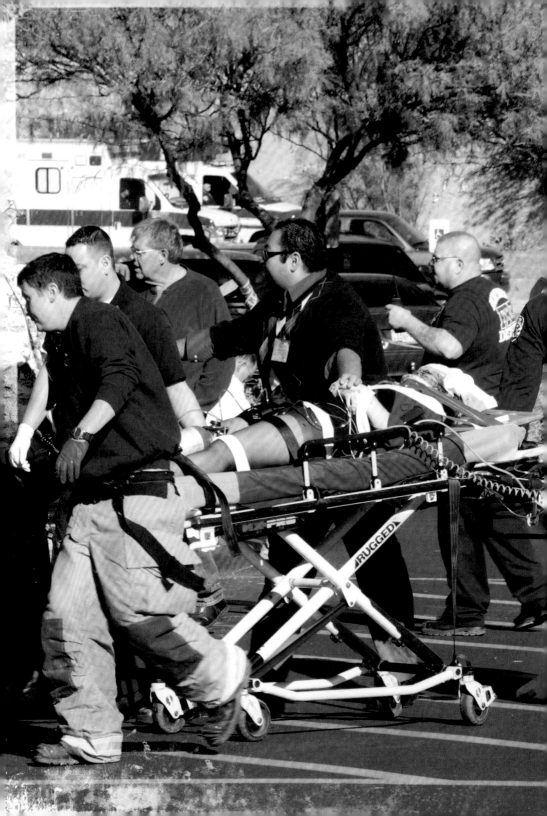

INTRODUCTION

The Gun-Control Debate

On THE MORNING OF JANUARY 8, 2011, A SMALL crowd gathered at a supermarket in Casas Adobes, Arizona. People had come to see U.S. representative Gabrielle Giffords, who was holding a public meeting there. Many simply wanted to meet their congresswoman. Others wanted to ask her questions. One man, twenty-two-year-old Jared Lee Loughner, had a different motive. He wanted to kill Giffords.

Loughner showed up at the meeting shortly after ten, carrying a semiautomatic pistol called a 9mm Glock. He marched past the crowd toward the table where Giffords sat. He raised the gun and fired a shot into Giffords's head before anyone could react. The shot struck Giffords near the left eye.

The violence didn't end there. As Giffords slumped to the ground, Loughner turned toward the crowd. His weapon held a magazine (ammunition-feeding device)

Left: Paramedics rush U.S. representative Gabrielle Giffords to the hospital after she was shot at a public appearance on January 8, 2011. The gunman killed six people and wounded thirteen, renewing the debate over gun rights in the United States.

with more than thirty bullets. Over the next fifteen seconds, Loughner sprayed bullets into the crowd, killing six people and wounding thirteen others. Giffords survived the attack, but she suffered severe trauma to her head and brain. Among the dead were nine-year-old Christina Taylor Green and federal judge John Roll.

The death toll could have been far worse. After Loughner emptied his first magazine, he tried to reload. But he dropped the second magazine. A bystander grabbed it while another clubbed Loughner in the head with a folding chair. Several others tackled Loughner and pinned him to the ground until the police arrived.

The shooting led to serious discussion around the nation. Some argued that Loughner's act was politically motivated. Others said it was a sad result of untreated mental illness. Many gun-control activists pointed to the incident as an example of the harm guns can do when they're inadequately regulated. Although Loughner's history showed that he had been in trouble with the law and was mentally unstable, he passed a background check and legally obtained a deadly semi-automatic weapon. Gun-rights supporters countered that Loughner, not his gun, was to blame for the shooting. He was a mentally ill young man who made a tragic choice.

The incident rekindled a debate that has raged for decades. What gun rights should U.S. citizens have? Should anyone be able to own powerful firearms, or should the government limit gun rights? Are guns a danger to society, or do they protect us from criminals and help guarantee freedom for all?

THE RIGHT TO KEEP AND BEAR ARMS

Gun control is a complex and hotly debated issue in the United States. The U.S. Constitution, a document that defines the basic principles and laws of the United States, guarantees all Americans the right to keep and bear arms. But what does this really mean? What did the founders intend when they wrote this guarantee more than two hundred years ago? And how does it apply to modern society and high-tech weaponry?

No one denies that a gun in the wrong hands can be deadly. In the United States, about thirty thousand people die each year as a result of gunshot wounds. This figure includes murders, suicides, and accidents.

Proponents of gun control say that the issue is simple: More guns in society cause more gun-related deaths. They say that children, criminals, and people with serious mental illness shouldn't have easy access to guns.

Gun-rights supporters often counter this argument by saying that guns don't kill people—people kill people. They mean that guns are nothing but tools. The shooters—not their guns—are to blame for gun-related deaths. They also point out that millions of gun owners are law-abiding citizens. They use guns only for hunting, target shooting, and self-defense, and they take many safety precautions.

How can society preserve its responsible citizens' right to own weapons while keeping guns away from dangerous people? That's the crux of the gun-control debate, and there are no easy answers.

USA TODAY Snapshots®

Countries with high gun ownership rates

Among 178 countries surveyed, those with the highest ownership rates of small arms — from handguns to semiautomatic rifles: (Rate per 100 civilians)

USA — 89
Yemen — 55
Switzerland — 46
Finland — 45
Serbia — 38

Source: 2007 Small Arms Survey, a research organization based in Switzerland

By Anne R. Carey and Alejandro Gonzalez, USA TODAY, 2008

CHAPTER ONE

Building a Culture of Guns

THE ISSUE OF CONTROLLING WEAPONS ISN'T NEW—nor is it unique to the United States. People have argued over it for centuries.

For example, in the 1100s, a debate raged in Europe over weapons called crossbows. A crossbow is a mechanized bow that fires short, heavy, pointed projectiles called bolts. It is much more deadly than an ordinary bow that fires arrows. In 1139 high-ranking Catholic clerics met in Rome, Italy. This meeting was called the Second Lateran Council. Some historians think that this council banned the crossbow. The clerics described it as "a weapon hateful to God" and "too lethal for Christians to use against one another." Despite this condemnation, European armies—Christian and otherwise—continued to use the crossbow.

People began to use modern firearms such as cannons and guns in the 1300s. Early firearms used gunpowder, an explosive chemical mixture, to launch small projectiles from tubelike enclosures. Such

Left: Crossbows like these modern replicas were a big advance in medieval warfare. Some people at the time thought crossbows were too brutal and wanted them banned.

firearms originated in China and then spread to the Middle East and Europe.

Early on, the gun was mainly a curiosity. Guns were unreliable and inaccurate. Their range was short, and loading them was time-consuming. Gunpowder required careful handling. If its components separated or were unevenly distributed inside a gun, the gunpowder wouldn't explode, rendering the weapon useless. Proven weapons such as blades and bows were much more reliable and efficient.

EVOLVING GUNS, EVOLVING ATTITUDES

For centuries guns remained a fringe technology. They simply weren't reliable enough for use on the battlefield. But people continued to experiment with and improve on gun design. They also developed new

Above: This nineteenth-century French painting shows a fourteenth-century battle between King John II of France and Edward, the Black Prince, from England. For many decades after firearms became available, soldiers continued to use more reliable weapons such as swords and spears.

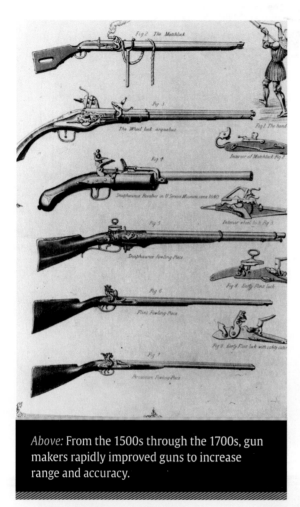

ineffective. Seasoned warriors scoffed at guns, seeing them as crude and clumsy. Many people viewed gun users as cowards. A true warrior relied on his blade—a weapon that required both skill and courage. Using a gun required little skill and even less courage, critics said.

Although guns and their users earned little respect for centuries, improving technology eventually made them impossible to ignore. From the 1500s through the 1700s, gun design advanced rapidly. Long-barreled guns called muskets brought greater range and accuracy. Fitted with blades called bayonets, muskets became useful for both long-range and close combat. Soon armies could not survive without guns. Firearms changed warfare permanently.

methods of preparing gunpowder, such as baking it into pellets. These methods improved gunpowder's reliability.

By the 1500s, pistols (handguns) and long guns such as the harquebus were common. Yet guns were still largely

While guns earned grudging acceptance as a military necessity, they remained unacceptable in civilian (nonmilitary) society. European aristocrats (ruling class) saw guns as a threat to their power. If common people had guns, they could easily revolt against their rulers. For this reason, many European nations strictly controlled guns. In 1594, for example, Queen Elizabeth I of England banned a type of gun called the wheel-lock pistol because it was easy to hide and to carry loaded.

In truth, many of these gun restrictions were unnecessary. At that time, guns were very expensive and difficult to use. A fear of the poor arising en masse (all together) with guns in hand was unrealistic. Few people could afford guns, and fewer still knew how to load and fire them. The restrictions didn't do much, in practical terms. But they did establish a social precedent (model). Those in power usually wanted to keep guns away from the common people.

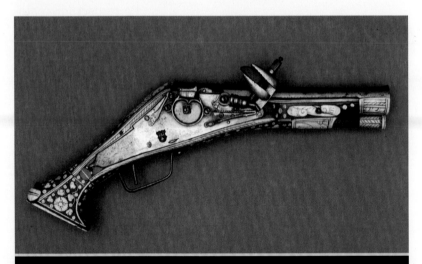

Above: In the late 1500s, England's Queen Elizabeth I banned the wheel-lock pistol because it was too easy to hide. This wheel-lock pistol was made in the early 1600s.

GUNS IN NORTH AMERICA

As gun technology evolved, new frontiers opened to Europeans. European colonists (explorers, soldiers, and settlers) began flocking to the Americas in the 1500s. England, France, Spain, Portugal, and other European nations sent shiploads of people across the Atlantic Ocean. Each nation was determined to grab and hold land in the Americas. Some of the colonists came armed with guns.

As wealth in the Americas grew and the cost of guns fell, a culture of guns developed there that had never existed in Europe. To many colonists, guns were a necessity. The Americas of the 1500s and 1600s were an unknown and dangerous place for Europeans. They had moved into a region already peopled by Native Americans. Europeans and Native Americans frequently clashed and fought over land. Colonists defended themselves with guns, and gun ownership became a way of life.

As Europeans expanded their settlements into the

Below: Guns were a part of life in colonial North America. Colonists depended on guns for food and defense. This drawing from the late 1800s shows early American settlers walking through a forest with a gun in hand for defense.

Americas, they drove out Native Americans—often violently. Firearms played a key role in this conquest. Gun-wielding Europeans had an advantage over Native Americans bearing bows, clubs, spears, and knives. Soon many Native American peoples wanted guns of their own, and firearms became an important article of trade between colonists and Native Americans.

By the 1700s, thirteen British colonies (dependent territories) dominated the eastern seaboard of North America. Citizens of these colonies lived under the British king's rule, but their lives were quite different from those of their fellow subjects in Great Britain. Gun ownership was one of many differences. In Europe guns remained restricted to society's elite. Laws still prevented common people from owning or using firearms. But in the early years, British rulers encouraged gun ownership among North American colonists. They did this for two reasons. First, the colonists weren't a direct threat to their rulers across the ocean. Second,

armed colonists could defend themselves. They didn't require British troops to keep them safe. The British Empire saved huge amounts of money by letting North American colonists defend themselves.

While gun ownership was widespread in North America, it wasn't unregulated. For example, in some colonies, able-bodied men who refused to serve in militias (small, local, loosely organized military groups) could not own weapons. Black slaves and other minorities could not carry firearms in any colony. A 1723 Virginia law read, "No negro [African American], mulatto [mixed-race person], or Indian [Native American] whatsoever . . . shall hereafter presume to keep, or carry any gun, powder, shot, or any club, or other weapon whatsoever, offensive or defensive." Such laws helped keep power in the hands of white people.

THE AMERICAN REVOLUTION

Throughout the 1700s, the thirteen colonies grew more self-sufficient and resentful of British interference. Meanwhile, Great Britain was fighting the French and several Native American peoples over territory along the western frontier of the colonies. This conflict was called the French and Indian War (1754–1763). Great Britain looked for ways to pay for its military expenses. The solution: higher taxes on the colonists.

The tax increase did not go over well in the colonies. Anti-British sentiment grew into widespread protests. Colonists complained that Great Britain was taxing them without giving them any say in British lawmaking. By contrast, their fellow citizens in Great Britain had some say in British government.

In the 1770s, tensions reached a breaking point. Fighting broke out in 1775, and the thirteen colonies banded together and declared independence from Great Britain in 1776. They formed a new nation, the United States of America, and rejected British rule of any kind. Great Britain would not let its colonies go without a fight. And so the American Revolution (1775–1783) began.

Above: Colonial militia members grab their guns and run to fight the British in the 1770s. The colonial army depended on local militias who had their own weapons.

The colonies' gun culture played a major role in the war. The fledgling United States had no stockpiles of weapons for its new military force, the Continental Army. So many Continental soldiers fought with their own weapons. Militias had fallen into disuse during the French and Indian War, which had brought many British troops to North America. But when the Revolutionary War began, militias re-formed across the colonies. They consisted of nothing more than local men, many of whom owned guns. These militias contributed to the fight against the British.

For these reasons, many early Americans celebrated gun ownership not only as a U.S. citizen's right but also as a citizen's obligation. Owning a gun was an act of patriotism. Guns became a symbol of the young United States' fierce independence.

Supplying U.S. troops with guns was a constant struggle for General George Washington, leader of U.S. forces, and his officers. While many people owned guns, most of them were in bad condition and were unsuitable for military use. This was especially true in frontier areas. Because of this gun shortage, U.S. troops often carried other weapons instead, such as bows, spears, and hatchets. Later in the war, guns imported from Europe helped turn the tide in the Continental Army's favor.

Washington didn't have enough guns to supply his whole army until the early 1780s, and victory came as soon as he did. U.S. troops forced a British surrender in 1781, ending the war in North America. A formal peace treaty followed in 1783.

A new nation was born. It was time to lay out the law of the land.

GUN LAWS IN THE NEW NATION

The young U.S. government and state governments had many decisions to make. Gun policy was one important issue they tackled.

After the war, the United States was full of guns and people who knew how to use them. Some leaders favored laws like those in Europe, which limited

gun rights. Others pointed to the role played by private citizens—and their guns—in the war. These leaders argued that all Americans should have the right to bear arms.

Senator Rufus King of New York fell into the camp that supported gun control. In 1790 he argued before the U.S. Senate "that it was dangerous to put arms into the hands of the frontier people for their defense, lest they should use them against the United States." This opinion had some justification. The young U.S. government had already faced rebellions, including Shays' Rebellion a few years earlier. In that incident, poor farmers in western Massachusetts had taken up arms against the courts and tax collectors.

Others took the opposite view. Among them was Virginia politician Thomas Jefferson, who wrote, "What country can preserve its liberties if their rulers are not warned from time to time that their people preserve the spirit of resistance? Let them take arms. . . . The tree of liberty must be refreshed from time to time with the blood of patriots and tyrants." Jefferson was saying that an armed citizenry was

Above: Rufus King, a founder of the United States as well as a New York senator, was one of the first U.S. politicians to support gun control.

a way to guard against tyranny (cruel and oppressive government) in the young nation.

Gun rights eventually found their way into federal (national) and state laws. Many of these laws focused more on the government's right to call and arm militias than on personal gun rights. But they set an important legal precedent on the issue of gun control.

The most famous U.S. gun law is the Second Amendment to the Constitution. The United States adopted its Constitution in 1787, but many lawmakers and citizens were dissatisfied with the document. It lacked language to guarantee certain personal freedoms. So lawmakers added ten amendments, or changes, to the Constitution in 1791. These amendments, called the Bill of Rights, describe the specific rights of U.S. citizens. The Bill of Rights prevents the government from denying important individual freedoms. The Second Amendment reads:

> A well regulated Militia, being necessary to the security of a free State, the right of the people to keep and bear Arms, shall not be infringed.

❝ In all the discussions and debates, from the Revolution to the eve of the Civil War [1861–1865], there is precious little evidence that advocates of local control of the militia showed an equal or even a secondary concern for gun ownership as a personal right. ❞

–DON HIGGINBOTHAM, UNIVERSITY OF NORTH CAROLINA HISTORY PROFESSOR AND AUTHOR, 2005

> " **Revisionists [those with new interpretations] have gone beyond overinterpretation of the [Second Amendment's] preamble [introduction]. . . . If the framers of the Bill of Rights *had* wanted to distinguish a right that applied only to states and their ability to form militias, they clearly knew how to differentiate between 'people' and 'states.'** "
>
> —**BRIAN DOHERTY,** POLITICAL AUTHOR AND EDITOR, 2008

The wording of the Second Amendment is not entirely clear. Many historians note that militias were the key issue in this amendment. They believe the law's intention was to allow militias to exist. The young United States did not have a standing army. Militias provided the nation's only organized defense. Protecting the nation's right to call militias to arms was important. For these reasons, some people suggest that the Second Amendment refers to the public's collective right to own arms, not to individual gun rights.

Other historians focus on the phrase "the right of the people to keep and bear Arms." They believe this phrase suggests that the Second Amendment was to guarantee all citizens the right to own whatever guns they want. The preamble (introduction) about militias is irrelevant, they say.

EVOLVING GUN LAW

For a century after the Bill of Rights passed, Americans largely ignored the Second Amendment. Gun technology changed little during that time, and the nation didn't need further gun legislation.

Then, in 1873, an election dispute erupted in Louisiana. A white mob, angry at the results of a local election, attacked a group of African Americans protecting the courthouse in the town of Colfax. The African Americans were armed but badly outgunned. After a brief fight, they threw down their arms and surrendered. The white mob murdered almost all the African Americans.

Local authorities refused to bring murder charges against the white men. So the federal government charged the men with violating the Second Amendment rights of the African Americans they'd disarmed. The court found the white defendants guilty, but they appealed the decision. Their appeal went to the nation's highest court, the U.S. Supreme Court.

Below: This drawing from an 1873 edition of *Harper's Weekly* shows African Americans gathering their dead after the massacre in Colfax, Louisiana. The killings led to a legal case based on the Second Amendment that made it to the U.S. Supreme Court.

The James Gang Goes Down

On September 7, 1876, Jesse James and his gang robbed a bank in Northfield, Minnesota. The notorious gang shot the bank teller before grabbing the cash and starting their getaway. But the James gang had a problem. Word of the robbery had spread quickly through Northfield. Many of the townspeople had rushed to get their guns, and they were waiting outside the bank for the criminals to appear. The crowd of armed citizens shot every member of the gang, killing two of them. This event and others like it fueled the sentiment that people need guns for self-defense, so individual gun rights should be absolute.

Above: Members of the James gang pose for a picture with their weapons in the 1870s.

In its decision *United States v. Cruikshank*, the Court ruled that the Second Amendment only forbids the federal government from infringing upon the right to bear arms. The Court said that the amendment doesn't forbid individuals or groups from disarming others. The Court overturned the white men's convictions.

The absolute right of U.S. citizens to own guns went unchallenged for the next half century.

Meanwhile, gun technology came a long way. By the 1920s, guns were no longer the inaccurate, slow-loading beasts of centuries past. Long-barreled rifles shot spinning bullets with stunning accuracy. People could carry pocket-size handguns and fire them at a moment's notice. And automatic weapons let users fire multiple rounds of ammunition with a single pull of the trigger. Meanwhile, organized crime was on the rise.

Above: A police officer displays weapons taken from gangs in Chicago, Illinois, in the 1920s. Technology had led to improvements in existing guns and ammunition and the introduction of automatic guns.

Many legislators believed it was time for gun laws to catch up with gun technology.

The U.S. Congress passed its first law restricting guns in 1927. The Mailing of Firearms Act outlawed the shipping of concealable handguns by U.S. mail. The law's main purpose was to slow mail-order gun sales to members of organized crime groups. It was a small step—largely unopposed and easily skirted by criminals. Yet it marked the beginning of a new era of gun-control efforts.

EARLY GUN-CONTROL EFFORTS

Public fear about organized crime continued into the 1930s. Crime groups were growing ever bigger and bolder, using weapons of terrible power: sawed-off shotguns that could be hidden inside a coat, tommy guns (lightweight machine guns), and more. Criminals often outgunned the police, imperiling both the police and the public.

In 1934 the U.S. Congress proposed new legislation to deal with the problem. The National Firearms Act taxed the sales of certain weapons, including handguns, short-barreled rifles and shotguns, automatic weapons, silencers, and explosive devices. It also required registration of all such weapons with federal authorities. This was where the gun-control debate really began. Few opposed the regulation of automatic weapons and bombs, but the inclusion of handguns in the proposed law set off a firestorm of protest. The National Rifle Association (NRA), a gun-rights group founded in 1871, organized a letter-writing campaign objecting to that portion of the bill. It worked. Congress altered the law, leaving handguns out of it.

The National Firearms Act of 1934 proved ineffective at controlling gun violence. So four years later, Congress tried again. It introduced the Federal Firearms Act of 1938 as a more comprehensive gun-control bill. The original draft called for the registration of all guns and the licensing of gun owners. Supporters argued that the bill did not infringe upon the Second Amendment.

The National Rifle Association

During the Civil War, two Union (Northern) officers, William Church and George Wingate, were shocked by their troops' poor marksmanship (shooting accuracy). So in 1871, the two men formed the National Rifle Association (NRA) to promote rifle shooting and improve U.S. marksmanship.

The early NRA bore little resemblance to the political organization it would later become. It focused on building shooting ranges and promoting sport shooting. In the first decade of the 1900s, the NRA began encouraging youth shooting programs and college rifle clubs.

In 1916 the NRA took control of a firearms interest magazine, *Arms and the Man*. In 1923 the NRA changed the magazine's name to the *American Rifleman*. One purpose of the magazine was to inform NRA members of gun laws being discussed around the nation.

In 1934 the NRA formed its Legislative Affairs Division to fight perceived attacks on Second Amendment rights. This new wing of the NRA helped organize protests and letter-writing campaigns to pressure politicians into voting down laws restricting gun ownership.

The NRA's political clout grew over the following decades. Through the late 1960s, the organization supported some level of gun control. But passage of the Gun Control Act of 1968 created a rift among the NRA's leaders. Some supported modest gun control, and others opposed it in all forms.

By the mid-1970s, the latter viewpoint had prevailed, cementing the NRA's hardline stance. The NRA's lobbying power grew and grew. A 1999 survey of lawmakers and congressional staff named the NRA the nation's most powerful lobbying group. By the twenty-first century, the NRA had a national membership of nearly four million people.

It preserved the right to bear arms—with the proper documentation. But the NRA saw things differently. Once again, the organization protested loudly and effectively. Congress stripped the bill down. The version that passed accomplished several objectives. It banned the sale of firearms to convicted felons (people convicted of serious crimes) and fugitives (people on the run from the law). It outlawed the transport or shipping of firearms whose serial numbers had been removed or altered, making them difficult to track. And it barred unlicensed dealers from selling guns across state lines. This final part was a token gesture, however, as the cost of licensing was a paltry one dollar.

A REVIVED DEBATE

Throughout the 1930s, Americans struggled with the Great Depression, an international economic collapse (1929–1942). The United States joined World War II (1939–1945) in 1941. For the next four years, the nation was dedicated to the war effort. This effort gave the economy a much-needed jump start. Organized crime declined, and the gun-control debate quieted.

The debate reemerged in 1963. Senator Thomas Dodd of Connecticut sat on a U.S. Senate

Above: Senator Thomas Dodd speaks during a U.S. Senate hearing in the 1960s on the control of firearms.

committee that dealt with crime among youth. He blamed easy access to cheap imported handguns for contributing to the problem. He proposed making these cheap handguns more difficult and expensive to get by heavily taxing imported handguns. But perhaps Dodd had an additional motive. Dodd's home state, Connecticut, was a hub of gun manufacturing. Dodd's proposal would have helped U.S. gun manufacturers, who were losing sales to foreign gun makers.

Shortly after Dodd made his proposal, a tragedy shook the nation. Lee Harvey Oswald assassinated President John F. Kennedy in Dallas, Texas, on November 22, 1963. Oswald had used an imported Italian rifle. He had ordered the inexpensive rifle after seeing an advertisement in the NRA's magazine, the *American Rifleman*. Dodd responded by widening

the scope of his bill to include mail-order rifles and handguns. Congress defeated the bill, largely because many thought it was too sweeping.

Five years later, Congress passed the Gun Control Act of

Above: Lee Harvey Oswald stands outside his home in 1963 holding the weapon he used to kill President John F. Kennedy.

Left: Senato[...] Hotel in Los Angeles, California, [...] fter the speech. *Right:* Marti[n...] before he was assassinated [...]

1968. This act was a response to a series of violent urban riots and political assassinations, including the murders of civil rights leader Martin Luther King Jr. and Senator Robert Kennedy of New York, John Kennedy's brother. This legislation, unlike the bills before it, had some teeth. It severely restricted gun and ammunition sales across state lines. It required gun dealers to keep detailed records of every sale. It banned the import of guns not used for sporting purposes such as hunting or target shooting. It established a federal regulatory agency. This group later became the Bureau of Alcohol, Tobacco, Firearms and Explosives (ATF). The Gun Control Act of 1968 was the first comprehensive gun legislation ever passed in the United States.

The act was controversial. Some felt that comprehensive gun legislation was long overdue and that this law was just a beginning. Others claimed it infringed on Americans'

Second Amendment rights. The debate raged even within the NRA. One top NRA official reportedly favored the legislation. Others opposed it. The divide created a power struggle within the organization. Some members wanted to support reasonable gun control, while others opposed gun-control legislation of any kind. Eventually the latter group took control of the organization. Opposition to all gun control has remained the NRA's position ever since.

POLITICAL TUG-OF-WAR

Over the following decades, the issue of gun control became more and more political. The NRA grew into a large and powerful force. It used its size and wealth to lobby for eased restrictions on gun sales. (Lobbying is trying to influence public officials.) In elections the NRA usually supported conservative candidates, forcing a divide between conservatives (mostly Republicans) and liberals (mostly Democrats) on the issue.

In the early 1980s, controversy surrounded armor-piercing bullets. These bullets are specially designed to blast through armor, such as a bulletproof vest. Some people call such bullets "cop killers." Congress introduced bills to ban the sales of such bullets, but the NRA fought the ban. It claimed the ban would limit hunters' ammunition choices. But even many of the NRA's longtime political allies questioned that claim. One senator reportedly asked when deer had

Above: A woman holds an armor-piercing bullet. Many Americans want restrictions on this type of ammunition.

started wearing body armor. In other words, the bullets were unnecessary for hunting and were used mainly to kill people, especially police officers. Congress reached a compromise in the Law Enforcement Officers Protection Act of 1985. The law forbade U.S. manufacture or import of armor-piercing ammunition except for government use.

In 1986 the NRA scored a major victory in its battle against gun control. That year, thanks largely to the NRA's persistence, the U.S. Congress passed the Firearm Owners' Protection Act. This law scaled back many of the 1968 restrictions placed on gun dealers. It lifted the ban on interstate sales. It more narrowly defined the term *gun dealer* so that dealer restrictions applied to fewer gun sellers. And it allowed licensed dealers to sell at gun shows. In an attempt to balance these changes, the law banned machine guns made after 1986.

Other laws were in the works too. For example, two U.S. senators sponsored a bill called the Undetectable Firearms Act of 1988. If passed, this law would have banned all-plastic guns, which can evade metal detectors. The bill never came to a vote.

THE BRADY BILL

The next major gun-control debate started in 1987, when the Brady Handgun Violence Prevention Act was introduced in Congress. This proposal stemmed from the attempted assassination of President Ronald Reagan six years earlier. John Hinckley Jr. had opened fire on Reagan and others near a hotel in Washington, D.C. Reagan took a bullet in his lung but recovered quickly. His press secretary, James Brady, wasn't so lucky. A bullet struck him in the head. The bullet was designed to shatter on impact. It did, sending metal fragments into Brady's brain. Brady survived the attack, but the wound left him with a permanent brain injury and partial paralysis.

Later, Brady and his wife led a new campaign for gun control. They formed an organization

Above: Security forces launch into action after John Hinckley Jr. fired shots at President Ronald Reagan in 1981. On the ground with bullet wounds are Secret Service agent Timothy McCarthy; Washington, DC, police officer Thomas Delahanty; and White House press secretary James Brady.

called the Brady Campaign to Prevent Gun Violence. In the 1980s, its members lobbied for a gun-purchase waiting period. They proposed that anyone buying a gun should have to wait a set period before receiving the gun. They argued that a waiting period would prevent people from rushing out in anger or confusion to buy guns and commit crimes. It would also give police time to do background checks and prevent convicted felons and illegal immigrants from buying guns. The Bradys and their supporters asked for a seven-day waiting period.

The NRA protested. It claimed that a waiting period would not prevent violent criminals from obtaining guns. The NRA pointed out that criminals often buy guns from individuals, not from licensed gun dealers. The waiting period, the organization argued, would do little more than inconvenience law-abiding gun owners.

After a long and heated debate, the Brady Act finally passed—with some alterations—in 1993. The seven-day waiting period shrank to five days. And the waiting-period requirement would expire in 1998. Meanwhile, the Federal Bureau of Investigation (FBI) would set up an instant background check system to be used after the waiting period expired in 1998.

President Bill Clinton *(right)* signs the Brady Act, named after former White House press secretary James Brady *(left)*. Brady was shot during an assassination attempt on President Ronald Reagan in 1981.

The Columbine Shootings

On the morning of April 20, 1999, students and teachers filled the halls of Columbine High School in Columbine, Colorado. For most of them, the day started like any other. But later that morning, as gunshots rang through the school, the day became one that the world probably will never forget.

The shooters were two Columbine students, Eric Harris and Dylan Klebold. Harris and Klebold were later described as social outcasts at the school. They had been in trouble with the law before. They'd made threats against classmates and committed other petty (minor) crimes.

The boys fantasized about launching a massive attack on their school. They were too young to purchase firearms legally. So they enlisted help. An older friend attended a December 1998 gun show and bought a semiautomatic rifle and two shotguns for the boys. (Rifles and shotguns are long guns shot from the shoulder.) Another contact later sold them a semiautomatic handgun. The boys also built a cache (hidden supply) of homemade explosive devices at their homes.

Above: These are the guns and ammunition clips used by Eric Harris and Dylan Klebold in the 1999 Columbine shootings.

Above: Members of the Columbine community gather to remember the people gunned down on April 20, 1999. The shooting brought about passionate debate over gun control in the United States.

In the late morning of April 20, Klebold and Harris carried out their attack. They first tried to detonate bombs in the cafeteria, but the bombs did not explode. Next, they carried their firearms inside and opened fire. The boys killed one teacher and twelve students and injured another twenty-one students. Harris and Klebold ended their shooting spree by taking their own lives.

The story made news worldwide. Questions swirled. What had caused these boys to make such a terrible choice? And how had they acquired such powerful firearms?

The boys were too young to legally own these guns. Each had a history of criminal behavior. Both had undergone psychological treatment for emotional problems. Every warning sign was up, yet the boys managed to obtain deadly weapons. Gun-control activists quickly portrayed the tragedy as evidence that U.S. gun laws were too lax. If these boys could obtain that many powerful firearms, anyone could get them. Gun-rights supporters, meanwhile, took a different approach. They pointed out that existing gun-control laws hadn't prevented Harris and Klebold from getting the guns they wanted. More laws would do no good.

THE DEBATE CONTINUES

In 1994, just one year after the Brady Act passed, the gun-control debate reemerged over assault weapons (automatic or semi-automatic weapons designed for military-type attacks). That year Congress passed the Violent Crime Control and Law Enforcement Act. Among other things, this law banned many of the world's most common assault weapons by name. This part of the law became known as the Federal Assault Weapons Ban. The ban expired in 2004, and Congress declined to renew it. Since then proposals for new assault weapons bans have come and gone, but none has passed.

The gun-control debate heated up again in 2007 and 2008. A few years earlier, citizens of Washington, D.C., had mounted a legal challenge against the city's gun-control law. This law banned most residents from owning handguns, automatic firearms, high-capacity semiautomatic weapons, and unregistered firearms. The law also required firearms in the home to be unloaded, disassembled, or locked. The case, called *District of Columbia v. Heller*, rose all the way to the U.S. Supreme Court. The key question in this case was whether the Second Amendment protects individual gun rights or Americans' collective gun rights.

In June 2008, the Supreme Court reached a decision. It ruled, "The Second Amendment protects an individual right to possess a firearm unconnected with service in a militia, and to use that arm for traditionally lawful purposes, such as self-defense within the home." Therefore, the Washington, D.C., law violated the Second Amendment rights of the city's residents. The NRA and other gun-rights supporters hailed this ruling as a major victory.

The debate didn't end there, however—far from it. Gun-control supporters and gun-rights supporters clashed again after the January 2011 assassination attempt on Gabrielle Giffords. The ease with which Jared Loughner had carried out this shooting spooked citizens and lawmakers alike.

Some lawmakers said the shooting illustrated the need to loosen gun-control laws. They argued that public officials should be allowed to carry concealed weapons wherever they go. Others argued that Loughner—not his gun—was the problem. "It's not that the gun was evil," said Arizona congressman Trent Franks, "it's that it was in the hands of an evil person. [Giffords] was shot by some monstrous degenerate." The NRA, meanwhile, said the focus after the shootings should be on treating mental health issues, not on restricting gun ownership.

Others felt that the tragedy in Arizona showed a need for tightening gun laws. U.S. representative Peter King—a longtime gun-rights supporter—proposed a law making it illegal to carry a gun within 1,000 feet (305 meters) of a federal official. President Barack Obama wrote an editorial in the Arizona Daily Star, arguing that someone with Loughner's background should never have been able to buy a firearm. Obama called for stricter enforcement of existing gun laws and for improvements in the way states report data to the system used in background checks.

The debate rages on. Gun control is an issue that continues to divide Americans. Where should the government draw the line between individual rights and the safety of society? This question isn't going away anytime soon.

> **I believe that if common sense prevails, we can get beyond . . . stale political debates to find a sensible, intelligent way to make the United States of America a safer, stronger place.**

—PRESIDENT BARACK OBAMA, MARCH 14, 2011

Justices lean to extending gun owners' rights

From the Pages of USA TODAY During spirited arguments Tuesday, the Supreme Court appeared ready to rule that the Second Amendment right to bear arms covers gun regulations in states and cities.

Several key justices, including Anthony Kennedy, signaled they believe the right to firearms is sufficiently "fundamental" that it should cover people challenging state and local gun laws, as well as federal laws.

Such a decision expanding the reach of the Second Amendment likely would set off new rounds of lawsuits targeting specific regulations across the country.

Tuesday's arguments in a dispute over a Chicago handgun ban flowed from a 2008 ruling in which the Supreme Court said for the first time that the Second Amendment protects an individual's right. The prevailing judicial view had been that it covers a collective right of state militia, such as a National Guard.

That 2008 case, *District of Columbia v. Heller*, applied only to laws by the U.S. government and its federal enclaves, such as Washington. Tuesday's case tested whether the right to bear arms is so fundamental to liberty that it also protects people against state and local laws.

The city of Chicago says the answer is no and that the Second Amendment significantly differs from other constitutional provisions because it is associated with dangerous weapons.

Justice Kennedy, who was in the majority in the 5–4 ruling in 2008 and is often a swing vote, said, "If (the right to bear arms) is not fundamental, then Heller is wrong." Kennedy said he believed the 2008 case rested on individuals' fundamental right to firearms.

Chief Justice John Roberts agreed, saying, "I don't see how you can read Heller and not take away from it the notion that the Second Amendment, whether you want to label it fundamental or not, was extremely important to the framers (of the Constitution) in their view of what liberty meant."

Justice Stephen Breyer, who dissented in Heller, was most vigorous in asserting that the Second Amendment should not be accorded the same status as other rights. "We are starting with a difference in purposes at the least," he said, suggesting that the right to weapons cannot be equated with free speech, for example. "Even if (city officials) are saving hundreds of lives, they cannot ban (guns)?" Breyer asked, skeptically.

Justice John Paul Stevens, who also dissented in Heller, suggested by his questions that the Second Amendment right should be limited in the states and that local legislators should have wide latitude to curtail firearms.

Chicagoans challenging the handgun ban include Otis McDonald, who lives on the city's far South Side and says he wants a handgun to protect his family.

Virginia lawyer Alan Gura, who was the lead lawyer in the 2008 case and represents McDonald, spent most of his time Tuesday arguing for specific legal grounds on which the Second Amendment would extend to states.

The Supreme Court has "incorporated" most of the first 10 amendments to the Constitution—the Bill of Rights—to apply to the states through a provision of the 14th Amendment that says no state shall infringe on "life, liberty or property without due process of law."

Yet Gura argued the court should extend the Second Amendment through a separate clause that says, "No state shall . . . abridge the privileges or immunities of citizens of the United States." His rationale, which would reverse past court rulings, received a chilly reception from many of the justices, including Antonin Scalia. Gura said in his brief that such grounds would "honor the 14th Amendment's true meaning."

Paul Clement, a former U.S. solicitor general under President George W. Bush, represented the National Rifle Association and urged the justices to rely on the 14th Amendment's due process guarantee for broader gun rights.

Defending Chicago's handgun ban, lawyer James Feldman said the right to bear arms is not fundamental, as is the right of free speech or free religious exercise. "Firearms, unlike anything else that is a subject of the Bill of Rights, are designed to injure or kill," he said.

—Joan Biskupic

CHAPTER TWO

A Question of Safety

ON FEBRUARY 24, 2005, DAVID HERNANDEZ ARROYO Sr. was scheduled to appear in court. He was accused of failing to pay child support to his ex-wife, Mirabel Estrada.

But Arroyo had other plans. He parked near the Tyler, Texas, courthouse and waited for Estrada. When Estrada and their twenty-two-year-old son, David Jr., arrived, Arroyo approached them. In his hands, he held a MAK-90 semiautomatic rifle. Arroyo lifted the weapon and opened fire. One shot hit Estrada in the head, killing her. Another hit David Jr. in the leg, knocking him to the ground.

Several police officers rushed to the scene. But armed only with pistols, they couldn't match Arroyo's firepower. Arroyo shot at the officers, wounding them.

Mark Wilson, who lived nearby, heard the gunshots. He quickly grabbed his .45 caliber pistol—which he had a permit to carry—and rushed to the scene. He

Left: These holes in a first-floor window of the Smith County Courthouse in Tyler, Texas, are evidence of David Hernandez Arroyo's 2005 shooting spree.

found Arroyo standing with his weapon aimed at David Jr. Wilson believed Arroyo was going to kill his son. So Wilson raised his pistol and fired.

The shot hit Arroyo in the back, causing him to stumble forward. But Arroyo was wearing a bulletproof vest, which protected him from serious injury. Arroyo turned and leveled his weapon at Wilson, who dove behind a truck.

The two men exchanged gunfire. Wilson again shot Arroyo, this time in the chest, but again, the bulletproof vest protected him. Eventually Arroyo shot Wilson, knocking him to the ground. Arroyo shot Wilson three more times, killing him.

Arroyo fled the scene, but police later killed him. The community hailed Wilson as a hero. His actions had prevented Arroyo from killing David Jr. and others.

DO GUNS PROTECT US OR ENDANGER US?

The Tyler incident and others like it raise complicated issues. Some say that lax gun laws allowed a dangerous man, Arroyo, to obtain a powerful semiautomatic weapon and use it on innocent people. Gun-control advocates say that such shootings prove that the United States needs stricter gun control.

Gun-rights supporters point to Wilson's actions. Wilson was a law-abiding citizen who exercised his Second Amendment right to keep and bear arms. Although he lost his own life, his actions saved at least one other person. Gun-rights supporters say that Wilson's story tells why it's so important to protect the gun rights of ordinary citizens.

The arguments for and against gun control often revolve around one central question: do guns in society make us safer or put us in danger?

Those who favor stricter gun control often claim that inadequate gun regulation makes the United States a dangerous place. They point to western Europe as proof. Western Europe is culturally and economically similar to the United States. And most western European countries have stricter gun laws. Their societies have far fewer guns per person than the United States has. Their rates of shooting deaths—both intentional and accidental—are also much lower. One study tallied the total number of gun deaths in one year among children and teens in the United States at more than five thousand. Only nineteen such deaths took place in Great Britain, where gun control is much tighter.

Gun-control supporters say that limiting the number of guns in society also limits the number of gun deaths that occur. When criminals and potential criminals have a harder time getting guns, everyone is safer. When children have less access to firearms, accidental shootings decrease.

Those who favor less gun control take the opposite viewpoint. They argue that law-abiding citizens with guns can prevent crime. When adults own guns, they can defend themselves and others from criminal attacks. Criminals have to consider the possibility of running into gun-wielding citizens, which reduces crime. Gun-rights groups point out that crimes such as robbery and assault occur more often

> **The U.S. level of lethal violence is far out of line with [the violence levels] of other industrialized nations. The fact that most of our lethal violence involves firearms lends credence [support] to the hypothesis that the prevalence [easy availability] of guns is a prime reason.**
>
> —DAVID HEMENWAY, DIRECTOR OF THE HARVARD INJURY CONTROL RESEARCH CENTER, 2006

in Europe than in the United States. They say this is proof that guns deter crime. In addition, an armed citizenry provides the nation with a collective defense against tyranny. Gun-rights advocates are quick to point out that in the American Revolution, armed citizens helped secure personal freedom for all.

Some gun-rights activists say Mexico's experience shows that excessive gun control doesn't work. Mexican citizens' gun rights are severely restricted. Mexico's gun-control laws are supposed to prevent drug traffickers and other criminals from arming themselves. But these criminals are heavily armed despite the laws. The restrictions keep guns from law-abiding citizens but do little to stop criminals from stockpiling them. Chris Cox, chief lobbyist for the NRA, says, "Mexico has very strict gun laws which clearly have done nothing to prevent criminals and drug cartels from obtaining

Below: Mexican police catalog the weapons taken after a shootout with drug traffickers in 2009. Although Mexico has strict gun-control laws, criminals often carry high-powered weapons.

firearms, and it's left many of the honest residents of Mexico defenseless."

Meanwhile, gun-control supporters—including Mexico's president, Felipe Calderón—note that Mexican gun laws don't work because U.S. gun laws are so lax. About 90 percent of the guns recovered in Mexico come from the United States. It's hard to buy a gun legally in Mexico. But it's easy to buy an illegal gun smuggled in from the United States.

Above: Mexican president Felipe Calderón appears at a ceremony in 2010. Calderón supports Mexico's gun-control laws—and blames the lax laws in the United States for Mexico's gun problems.

ACCIDENTAL SHOOTINGS

Criminal use of guns isn't the only danger, of course. Many gun-related deaths are accidents. A child may find an adult's loaded gun and play with it. A hunter may mistake another hunter for prey, accidentally fire a gun in the wrong direction, or injure someone with a stray bullet. Irresponsible teenagers may goof off with guns without really appreciating the danger they represent.

Firearms education and gun-safety classes can curb irresponsible adult gun use. But U.S. children face a great risk of accidental shooting. A 2005 study found that about 1.7 million U.S. children live in homes with loaded, unlocked guns. The same study concluded that about 90 percent of accidental shooting deaths among children occurred in the home.

Fearing liability (legal and financial responsibility) for such accidents, gun companies have started programs to give away millions of free gun locks. When engaged, these small devices prevent guns from firing, even when they're loaded.

Despite these measures, many children still have access to guns. How far should the government go to protect them?

Above: Many gun locks are available, such as this RAC lock, which can be used at home or in a vehicle *(inset).*

Above: While many gun advocates encourage the use of gun locks such as this, they believe gun locks should be voluntary.

Some gun-control advocates think that gun locks should be mandatory. Others suggest that the law should require technology that allows only a gun's owner to operate it.

The NRA and other gun-rights groups support the use of gun locks and other safety devices, but they believe that use should be voluntary. They say that laws forcing gun owners to use safety devices are a needless government intrusion on people's lives.

SUICIDES

Sometimes forgotten in the gun-control debate is the issue of suicide. More than half of all suicides in the United States are gun suicides. Suicide is the second-leading cause of death in the United States among people forty and younger. The suicide rate is especially high among teenagers. Teens are more easily overcome by depression and impulsiveness than are emotionally mature adults.

Most suicide attempts are unsuccessful. Drug overdose is the most common method of attempted suicide, and this method fails about 97 percent of the time. Suicide attempts involving firearms are a different story. About 90 percent of gun-related suicide attempts are successful. Studies show that suicide rates for adolescents who live in homes with guns are far higher than for those who live in homes without guns. Rates increase anywhere from two times to ten times, depending on factors such as age and gun storage methods. Researchers have concluded that suicide success rates correlate directly with access to firearms.

Suicide attempts are usually rash and impulsive. According to a study conducted at the Centers for Disease Control and Prevention (CDC), 24 percent of people who attempt suicide take less than five minutes to make their decision and 70 percent take less than one hour. David Hemenway, director of the Harvard School of Public Health's Injury Control Research Center, points out that failed suicide attempts don't necessarily lead to repeat attempts. "Studies show that most attempters act on impulse, in moments of panic or despair," Hemenway said. "Once the acute feelings ease, 90 percent do not go on to die by suicide."

However, people who use guns to attempt suicide hardly ever get a second chance. Many believe the United States needs tighter gun control to keep guns away from suicide-prone juveniles. In addition, gun-purchase waiting periods can reduce impulsive suicidal behavior in adults. A 2001 article in the *American Journal of Psychiatry* illustrates this point. A young man in New York was distraught after the end of a long relationship. He decided to take his own life. But because of New York laws, he couldn't buy a gun immediately. He had to wait for a license. So instead of buying a gun, the man sought psychological help. Restricted access to firearms probably saved his life.

Gun-rights supporters argue that guns are not the cause of

suicides but merely tools used in committing suicide. Even if guns are inaccessible, determined individuals have many other options for taking their own lives. Opponents of gun control further argue that law-abiding citizens should not have to give up gun rights to protect potential suicide victims. They point out that many more people die as a result of motor vehicle accidents than in suicides, but that doesn't mean we should ban motor vehicles.

SELF-DEFENSE

Gun owners cite three main reasons for owning guns: protection against crime (self-defense), target shooting, and hunting. The reason cited most often is self-defense. A gun can level the playing field between criminals and their potential victims. A homeowner with a gun can fend off a thief. An armed woman walking alone can use her gun to repel an attacker.

The number of defensive gun uses (DGUs) in the United

Above: Various types of firearms classes are available throughout the United States. These classes help gun owners avoid accidents caused by ignorance and panic. Classes show users how to use and store firearms safely.

States is hard to pin down. Gun-rights groups claim more than two million DGUs in the United States every year, based on polling data. Gun-control advocates say that the polling data is either flawed or fraudulent and that the real number of DGUs is far lower.

According to one study, about 1 percent of potential victims of violent crimes used guns to defend themselves. This percentage includes people such as police officers and security guards. The study didn't include people defending their homes from nonviolent offenders such as burglars.

Gun-control advocates point to this number as proof that Americans rarely use guns in

> **"The data shows that guns are used in . . . violent acts about 500,000 times a year. Guns are used defensively about four times that number, about 2 million times a year. And quite often, they're merely brandished, not even fired. The deterrent [preventive] purpose of guns, the possession of guns by people who want to defend themselves, is what we have to preserve and what now the Supreme Court has [told] us the Constitution does, in fact, preserve."**
>
> **—ROBERT LEVY,** CHAIRMAN, CATO INSTITUTE, 2009

self-defense. Meanwhile, gun-rights supporters argue that in many cases, when a citizen draws a weapon in self-defense, no violent crime happens—and the incident goes unreported. Therefore, many gun-rights supporters reject the usefulness of this data.

Some Americans wonder whether guns owned for self-defense do more harm than good. A 2009 University of Pennsylvania study found that a person carrying a gun is 4.5 times more likely to be shot than a person who does not carry one. Victims actively trying to use a gun for self-defense are still more likely to be shot. Gun-control advocates argue that guns provide a false sense of security while raising the risk of death or serious injury. Gun-rights activists counter that many people carry guns because they are already at a higher risk for violence. This fact, they say, skews the numbers. It invalidates the argument that carrying a gun in self-defense does more harm than good.

The use of firearms in self-defense brings up a related question: when is it acceptable to shoot at another human being? Most people agree that if a criminal poses an immediate threat to someone's life, extreme force is justified. But few incidents are so clear-cut. What about an unarmed burglar in one's home? Or someone vandalizing private property? Where do we draw the line between acceptable self-defense and unacceptable overkill? What responsibility does a citizen have to avoid a potentially lethal exchange?

Americans grappling with these questions fall into two main camps. One is the "stand your ground" camp. People in this camp believe that a person under threat has the right to stand his or her ground and fire at the offender. The other camp takes a "duty to retreat" approach. People in this camp believe that a person under threat must make every effort to remove him- or herself from the situation before firing. Only when all other options have failed should someone open fire on an attacker.

Taking up arms against intruders

From the Pages of
USA TODAY

Kathy Adkins moves from target to target, firing with deadly efficiency a .38-caliber revolver and then a 9mm semiautomatic pistol at human-shaped targets.

Adkins, 48, owns a real estate firm in nearby Jackson [Mississippi] and has been taking firearms training since March. Instructor Cliff Cargill says she's among the new students he has racked up since the Legislature passed a law last year giving citizens expanded legal rights to protect themselves in their homes, cars or businesses.

The "Castle Doctrine" law removes the requirement that citizens first must seek a safe retreat from an intruder before using deadly force. Similar laws have passed in 19 other states in two years, in large part because of lobbying by the National Rifle Association (NRA).

A recent spate of shootings in Jackson, the capital, has reinvigorated public discussion of the law. In one week in late September and early October, four Jackson homeowners fired shots at four suspected burglars. Two of the suspected intruders were killed and a third was injured.

Only one of the homeowners in those shootings—a convicted felon who is not allowed to own a firearm—faces criminal charges. Jackson police spokesman Cmdr. Lee Vance says virtually every local news account about the shootings mentioned the Castle Doctrine law.

"Whether it was a factor . . . or not, it's getting a lot of credit," he says.

That's what critics of the law and anti-gun advocates are afraid of. They say it promotes violence and weakens police powers.

Peter Hamm, spokesman for the Brady Campaign to Prevent Gun Violence, says the measure bucks a long trend in American law toward reduced public violence dating back to the taming of the West.

"Do we want to kill every 16-year-old kid we find stealing a car stereo?" he says.

The NRA says the principle behind the law is more basic. "We want to make sure that in America the right to self-defense continues to exist and that the American citizen's home remains his castle," says NRA Executive Vice President and CEO Wayne LaPierre.

While it might be too early to tell if the laws have had an impact on justifiable shootings, FBI statistics show 241 justifiable homicides [murders] by private citizens in 2006. That's a 23% increase over the previous year, but that is fewer than the 247 killed in 2003 before the NRA push began. Overall, Department of Justice records show a 13% decrease in justifiable homicides over the past decade.

Mississippi isn't the only state making news over the Castle Doctrine law.

Last week, Joe Horn, 61, of Pasadena, Texas, shot and killed two men that he told a police dispatcher were burglarizing his neighbor's home, according to a transcript of the tape.

Bill Delmore, legal services bureau chief for the Harris County District Attorney's office, says it is too early to speculate.

"One issue is going to be whether the so-called Castle Doctrine law applies to a neighbor's home," he says, adding that the state has other laws governing self-defense and the protection of property that might apply. A grand jury will decide if charges will be filed against Horn.

Also in Texas, the Associated Press reported in September that Dallas musician Carter Albrecht was shot and killed when he tried to kick in the door of his girlfriend's neighbor. The shooting happened just days after the state passed its Castle Doctrine law.

Dallas police Sgt. Larry Lewis says no charges are being pursued against the shooter.

Mike Snider, a Dallas concert promoter who knew Albrecht, says Albrecht had been arguing with his girlfriend and might have banged on the wrong door. "There is no excuse for blindly shooting a gun in anyone's direction," he says.

In all, the Brady Campaign has noted at least nine shootings they believe to be inspired by Castle Doctrine laws or prosecutions complicated by them.

George Washington University law professor Robert Cottrol says the Castle Doctrine law is a more incremental change than either side of the gun-control debate wants to admit. Realistically, he says, prosecutors have not been eager to prosecute people who truly act in self-defense.

"There is a fundamental feeling on the part of many that the aggressor should not profit and the person who is defending should not be held in legal jeopardy," he says.

—Chris Joyner

Castle Laws

Many U.S. states have adopted laws that permit citizens to defend themselves from intruders in their homes. Such laws are called castle doctrine laws, or simply castle laws. They're based on the idea that people have the right to defend their "castles" (their homes) and innocent people therein from illegal trespassing or violent attack.

Castle laws generally ignore the rule of minimum necessary force. They give citizens broad protection from criminal charges and civil lawsuits for using self-defensive violent force in their own homes.

Castle laws vary by state, and not all states have them. In some states, homeowners must verbally announce their intent to shoot before doing so, giving an intruder a chance to flee. Other states require no such warning.

U.S. laws on self-defensive gun use differ from state to state. However, most state laws contain some form of the following principle: a person who faces immediate danger from another person may use the minimum necessary force to secure his or her own safety.

What is the minimum necessary force? It's just enough force to prevent injury to yourself or someone you wish to protect, but no more. For example, if a mugger comes at you with a baseball bat, you could argue that firing a gun at him is a reasonable level of force. However, if you shoot the mugger and knock him to the ground, firing additional shots at him would be unnecessary. You could face charges for the additional shooting.

Technically, a person who shoots someone in self-defense may be arrested and called before a judge. The shooter must demonstrate how his or her actions were necessary for self-defense. If the judge finds that the shooter used more than

Above: Sharron Nicole Redmond testifies during her 2005 trial for the shooting death of her boyfriend. She was found not guilty because the jury believed she fired the gun in self-defense.

the minimum necessary force, the shooter could face a criminal trial. In practice, however, the U.S. justice system rarely prosecutes civilians in self-defense cases.

CHAPTER THREE

Who Should Own Guns?

IN 2010 A DEBATE ERUPTED IN THE U.S. CONGRESS AND on the national political stage. Americans were arguing over who should be allowed to own and carry guns in the United States. The basic issue was nothing new. But the specifics made people—even staunch gun-rights supporters—a little uneasy.

The question was simple: should suspected terrorists (people with ties to known terrorists, people who use violence to get their way) have the right to own and carry weapons? An FBI report had brought up the question. The report stated that from 2004 to 2010, more than eleven hundred suspected terrorists had legally bought firearms or explosives in the United States.

Laws already prevented suspected terrorists from boarding commercial airplanes. Airlines could not accept passengers whose names appeared on a

Left: Laws prevent suspected terrorists from traveling on commercial airplanes. Should laws also prevent certain people from owning guns?

national No Fly List (part of the FBI's Terrorist Watch List). But many people on the No Fly List could still buy firearms—as long as they weren't convicted felons or illegal immigrants. Many members of Congress wanted to change that. They wanted suspected terrorists added to the list of people who cannot legally buy firearms.

> ## Green light for gun buyers
> Under current law and procedures, most gun-purchase applications by people on the government's terrorist watch list are approved:
>
> **FBI-screened applicants from Feb. 3 to Oct. 30, 2004:**
> Watch-list applicants
> ||||||||||||||||||||||||||||||||||||||||||||||||| 35
> Purchases approved
> ||||||||||||||||||||||||||||||||||||||| 31
>
> **State-screened applicants[1] from Feb. 3 to June 30, 2004:**
> Watch-list applicants
> ||||||||||||||||||||||||||| 23
> Purchases approved
> ||||||||||||||| 16
>
> 1 –11 states were included in the GAO study
> Sources: U.S. Government Accountability Office (GAO); FBI
>
> By Alejandro Gonzalez, USA TODAY, 2005

Certain categories of people can't own guns in the United States, according to the Gun Control Act of 1968:

- people convicted in federal courts of crimes punishable by imprisonment for more than one year;
- people convicted in state courts of crimes punishable by imprisonment for more than two years;
- fugitives from justice;
- people who are unlawful users of or are addicted to drugs;
- people who have been declared in court as having a mental defect (illness or deficiency) or who have been committed to mental institutions;
- illegal immigrants and visitors to the United States, unless they possess a current valid hunting license;
- people dishonorably discharged from the U.S. armed forces;
- people who have given up their U.S. citizenship;
- people subject to restraining orders (court orders preventing them from harassing, stalking, or threatening others); and
- people convicted of domestic violence.

At first glance, the idea of keeping guns away from terrorists may seem like a no-brainer. Terrorists endanger all society. Many of them kill indiscriminately (without careful selection of victims) and without remorse.

But the matter isn't that simple. Some people on the Terrorist Watch List have not committed any serious crimes. The FBI merely suspects these people of being terrorists or of having close ties to terrorists. Can the government deny an individual's Second Amendment rights based solely on suspicion?

The U.S. Senate held a committee meeting to discuss proposed legislation that would add suspected terrorists to the list of people prohibited from owning guns. The debate was heated. It left people on both sides of the gun-control debate uncertain of where they stood.

The committee invited New York City's mayor, Michael Bloomberg, to speak in support of stricter measures. "If society

Above: New York City mayor Michael Bloomberg speaks on gun laws at City Hall on January 24, 2011. Bloomberg spoke up for better enforcement.

decides that these people are too dangerous to get on an airplane with other people, then it's probably appropriate to look very hard before you let them buy a gun," he said.

"But we're talking about a constitutional right here," countered South Carolina senator Lindsey Graham.

"The watch list can be inaccurate," Maine senator Susan Collins said. "It is not, in other words, equivalent of a criminal history report." In other words, being on the list does not necessarily mean one has actually done anything wrong.

NRA officials denounced the proposal as a sneaky plan to undermine the Second Amendment. They argued that the government could place names on the list as needed, snuffing out the Second Amendment rights of its critics. The proposal was unconstitutional, said the NRA. Some members of Congress agreed. They thought the plan would set a dangerous precedent. By early 2011, the proposed law had not been brought to a vote.

This debate is just one example within the larger debate over Americans' Second Amendment rights. Whom does the Second Amendment protect? Whom should it protect? When does a person forfeit his or her Second Amendment rights? Is it ever constitutional for the government to restrict gun rights?

INDIVIDUAL VERSUS COLLECTIVE GUN RIGHTS

The Second Amendment shows clearly that our nation's founders intended private gun ownership to be legal in the United States. But did they really mean it to be an absolute right of all Americans? Whatever the founders' intentions, most Americans agree that young children and violent criminals should not be allowed to have guns. But Americans disagree over the gun rights of other groups. Where should the line be drawn?

The answer to this question depends on how a person interprets the Second Amendment. Many believe it grants the citizenry merely a collective, or

> **We don't have strict enough standards for who should possess a gun, can legally possess a gun. But maybe more importantly, we really don't have systems that hold gun sellers accountable to make sure that they are only transferring guns to truly law-abiding people who are mentally competent.**
>
> —**DANIEL WEBSTER,** CODIRECTOR, JOHNS HOPKINS UNIVERSITY CENTER FOR GUN POLICY AND RESEARCH, 2009

group, right to keep and bear arms. They think the founders meant that society has the right—even the obligation—to own and use guns as a means of defense. Those who prefer this interpretation urge others to remember the situation of the young nation. The United States had little money. It could not afford to maintain a standing army. Foreign powers ruled the lands to the north, west, and south. Native Americans were in conflict with settlers. The founders wanted to ensure that the government could call upon local militias for national

defense. After all, in the preamble to the Second Amendment, the founders expressly mentioned the role of militias in national security. And they couldn't have meant to guarantee individual gun rights, because in their time, many people had no such rights. Slaves couldn't own guns. Violent criminals were quickly disarmed. Even the poor would have been prevented from owning guns, not by law but by poverty.

Other Americans interpret the Second Amendment differently. They focus on the latter part of the amendment's wording. They believe it grants individuals the right to keep and bear arms. Those who use this interpretation say that just as the First Amendment grants all individuals the right of free speech, so the Second Amendment grants all individuals the right of gun ownership. They say that if the government passes a law that prevents a citizen from owning guns, that law violates the Constitution.

This issue was at the heart of the 2008 U.S. Supreme Court case *District of Columbia v. Heller*. The Court ruled 5–4 that the Second Amendment grants individual gun rights. Explaining the Court's decision, Justice Antonin Scalia wrote, "Nowhere else in the Constitution does a 'right' attributed to 'the people' refer to anything other than an individual right. What is more,

Below: Dick Heller displays his newly approved gun permit outside the District of Columbia Police Department after the Supreme Court ruled in his favor in *District of Columbia v. Heller* in 2008.

in all six other provisions of the Constitution that mention 'the people,' the term unambiguously [clearly] refers to all members of the political community, not an unspecified subset."

Still, the verdict was not unanimous. Many gun-control supporters continue to believe that Americans should read the Second Amendment with the context of its writing in mind.

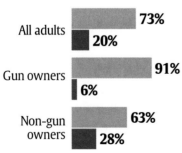

USA TODAY Gallup Poll ⊠

Do you believe the Second Amendment to the U.S. Constitution guarantees the rights of Americans to own guns, or does it only guarantee members of state militias such as National Guard units the right to own guns?

▮ **Right of all Americans**
▮ **Only state militas**

All adults
73%
20%

Gun owners
91%
6%

Non-gun owners
63%
28%

Source: USA TODAY/Gallup Poll of 1,016 adults Feb. 8–10. Margin of error for all adults: ±3 percentage points; for gun owners: ±6 points; for non-gun owners: ±4 points.

By Julie Snider, USA TODAY, 2008

WHY DO PEOPLE OWN GUNS?

To debate who should be permitted to own guns, we must understand why people might want to own guns. According to a 2005 Gallup Poll, 42 percent of Americans either own a gun or live with someone who does. Their reasons for gun ownership fall into five general categories.

1. Self-defense: About 67 percent of gun owners cite protection against crime as the reason. A single woman might carry a small handgun to ward off an attacker. Parents may keep a gun locked up at home to protect their family from intruders. Guns offer these people peace of mind. Police officers and security guards carry guns as part of their work defending public safety.

2. Sport shooting: Some people own guns so they can shoot at inanimate objects. About 66 percent of gun owners cite target shooting as a reason. These people enjoy the challenge of mastering

Above: Randall McLelland shoots during the qualifying round of men's skeet at the 2008 Beijing Olympics in China. Sport shooting is one of the main reasons people give for gun ownership.

their speed and accuracy with a gun. Skeet shooters fire at clay targets launched into the air. Some shooters fire at paper targets at gun ranges.

3. Hunting: About 58 percent of gun owners cite hunting as a reason. Hunting is a way of life for many Americans. They build vacations, weekends, and other free time around hunting trips. Some rely on hunting as a source of meat. Others just love the thrill of the hunt.

4. Gun collecting: Many people collect guns as a hobby. Some collect antique guns. Others collect the latest and greatest gun technology. Collectors often attend gun shows and proudly display their treasures. Many collectors rarely fire the guns in their collections.

5. Crime: Some people own guns for criminal reasons. For those in organized crime and for common thugs, guns are a guaranteed way to command attention and to wield power.

Most Americans agree that guns are acceptable for self-defense, hunting, sport shooting, and collecting, while they're unacceptable for crime. But it's impossible to protect all acceptable gun use without giving criminals easy access to guns. So Americans must decide: is it more important to guarantee the rights of law-abiding citizens or to prevent violence by denying criminals easy access to weapons? This is the essence of the U.S. gun-control debate.

CRIMINALS AND THE MENTALLY ILL

Regardless of whether the right to keep and bear arms is an individual right or a collective right, most people would agree that it should come with some restrictions. Foremost among those exceptions would be for criminals.

Below: Hunters head out on a morning hunt in North Dakota. Hunting is another top reason Americans give for owning guns.

Under U.S. law, people convicted of felonies cannot own guns or ammunition. Neither can a person convicted of a misdemeanor (lesser crime) domestic battery. (Domestic battery is violence against a person with whom one shares a close relationship, such as a family member, a roommate, a friend, a spouse, a girlfriend, or a boyfriend.) Individual states can restore this right in special cases. But most felons face severe penalties (up to ten years in prison) if caught with firearms, even at home.

Even these restrictions are a source of controversy. Some ex-criminals who have served their time and are rehabilitated (restored to a positive and useful place in society) argue that such restrictions infringe upon their constitutional rights. And some law-abiding citizens agree. They see the criminal restrictions as a slippery slope leading toward more restrictions. They point out that the Second Amendment says nothing about denying criminals the right to bear arms. Rather, the amendment guarantees this right for *all* people.

Furthermore, say gun-rights advocates, the law doesn't distinguish between different types of felonies. But all felonies are not equal in terms of danger to society. Should someone convicted of a nonviolent felony such as tax evasion (illegally avoiding tax payment) lose his or her Second Amendment rights? What about someone convicted of a crime in a foreign country with different laws or in a country that lacks the due process (system of fairly and systematically determining a person's innocence or guilt) to which U.S. courts adhere? Is it fair to strip these people of their gun rights?

Many gun-control advocates feel that protecting the rights of convicted criminals is far less important than protecting the safety of society at large. They argue that no felons or domestic abusers should have access to firearms. By committing crimes, these people have forfeited certain rights. Convicted felons may also lose the right to vote,

> **There already are 20,000 federal gun laws and regulations on the books. If those laws haven't made America safe by now, why should we think 20,001 laws will suffice? We shouldn't. Instead, we need to recognize that those 20,000 laws are a principal cause of the current violence in society. They have made our children and all innocent adults much less safe by disarming innocent citizens and encouraging armed criminals to take advantage of us. So it's time to face reality and repeal these laws—all of them.**
>
> **—HARRY BROWNE,** FORMER LIBERTARIAN CANDIDATE FOR U.S. PRESIDENT, 2000

hold office, or live in federally funded housing. Gun-control advocates say that losing the right to own guns is just part of the price criminals have to pay for their crimes.

Similar laws restrict gun ownership for individuals who have been legally declared as mentally deficient, as well as those who have been committed to psychiatric institutions. These laws are meant to keep guns away from people who don't have the mental capacity to use a gun responsibly, as well as those who have psychological disorders that could cause them to act out in antisocial ways or without fully understanding their actions. For example, a court may rule that a person with a mental illness such as schizophrenia (a condition in which a person becomes detached from reality) is too unpredictable to have a firearm.

In practice, denying gun rights for psychiatric reasons is difficult. Reporting of committals by psychiatric institutions has always been spotty. Many people who should, by law, be denied firearms have sailed through background checks. In addition, some people argue that the reporting of mental conditions raises serious questions about the privacy rights of mentally ill patients.

YOUTH AND GUNS

Young people also face gun ownership restrictions. In the United States, minors (children seventeen years and younger) don't have the same constitutional rights that adults have. Kids can't vote or buy alcohol. Their driving and employment privileges are limited. Likewise, minors can't buy firearms and ammunition. People twenty years old and younger can't buy handguns and handgun-only ammunition. Minors may own some guns with parental permission.

The reasons for restricting youth gun rights are straightforward. Many young people lack the knowledge and judgment needed to safely operate a firearm. The rate of accidental shooting deaths among kids is far higher than it is among adults. In addition, young people may not understand the full consequences of their actions. Their lack of intellectual and emotional maturity can lead to rash actions with guns, such as homicide and suicide.

Still, many minors do own guns—with their parents' permission—and know how to use them safely. Hunting is a way of life for many families in rural areas. Children in these families learn the proper handling of weapons from their parents and other responsible adults. Many states require minors to pass gun safety classes before using weapons.

The desire to keep guns out of the hands of children is a rare bit of common ground shared by both gun-control and

Are Gun Companies Responsible?

Some gun-control activists believe that gun manufacturers and dealers should be liable for damages incurred during gun crimes or gun accidents. They believe that the success of lawsuits against other companies, most notably tobacco companies, justifies this line of reason. Citizens suffering from the effects of smoking or breathing secondhand smoke have sued tobacco companies and collected money in damages. People have also sued the makers of a wide variety of other products that have proved deadly or harmful to consumers. Gun-control activists believe that any company should be held accountable if it makes a product that endangers consumers for any reason.

Gun companies and gun-rights activists oppose such lawsuits. They argue that as long as manufacturers and dealers sell their guns legally, they bear no responsibility for the actions of buyers.

In 2005 Congress passed the Protection of Lawful Commerce in Arms Act. This law shields gun manufacturers and dealers from lawsuits when they have sold guns legally and with no knowledge of a buyer's intent.

gun-rights advocates. But the two camps disagree on methods to control youth gun use. Many gun-rights supporters think that state or parental control is best. Gun-control supporters often favor more federal control and stricter penalties for those caught providing firearms illegally to children.

Despite questions about mental state, Cho could buy gun

From the Pages of
USA TODAY

Virginia State Police said Cho Seung Hui [who opened fire at Virginia Tech University in 2007, killing thirty-two people] could buy firearms legally even though he had once been ordered taken to a psychiatric hospital when he was reported to be suicidal.

Federal law bars gun purchases by anyone who has been deemed a "mental defective" by a court or ordered "committed to any mental institution."

Under the law, Cho didn't fall into either category, Virginia State Police said Wednesday. He was taken to a mental hospital for evaluation on Dec. 13, 2005. A friend had told police that Cho was suicidal after Cho had stalked female students at Virginia Tech, campus Police Chief Wendell Flinchum said.

The next day, a judge said Cho "presents an imminent danger to himself as a result of mental illness" but declined to commit him to a hospital, according to court documents. Instead, Cho was ordered to undergo outpatient psychiatric treatment.

When Virginia State Police reviewed Cho's March 12 application to buy a 9mm pistol at a Roanoke gun shop, "we determined he was eligible, and we approved him," said Donna Tate, program manager for the state police Firearms Transaction Center.

Virginia courts must notify state police when someone has been found mentally defective or committed to a psychiatric institution. "We have no such notification," Tate said.

A doctor who examined Cho at a Virginia psychiatric hospital found him depressed but not suicidal. "His insight and judgment are normal," the doctor said, according to court documents that were part of a file in which a judge declined to order Cho committed to the psychiatric hospital.

Cho's case has drawn attention to background checks that determine whether someone can legally buy a gun.

Federal law bars purchases by people convicted of serious crimes, drug addicts and illegal immigrants, according to the National Rifle Association. Also barred are people subject to restraining orders, convicted of domestic violence or who have renounced their citizenship or been dishonorably discharged from the military.

States typically provide records of convictions and other disqualifying incidents to FBI databases that are used for background checks.

But serious psychiatric problems that would disqualify a gun purchase may not always be found in background checks. About half the states don't report court psychiatric orders to the FBI, said Tom Bush, assistant director of the FBI's Criminal Justice Information Service. He said states are not required to report court psychiatric orders to the FBI. "States that submit do so voluntarily," Bush said.

States may not have the resources to transmit the orders, or may be prevented by state law from maintaining the orders in a way that they can be shared with other agencies, Bush said.

Dana Schrad, executive director of the Virginia Association of Chiefs of Police, said some states won't disclose psychiatric orders "because of privacy laws around mental health issues."

Some gun-control advocates say background checks should go beyond legal records and include a character assessment that would include interviews with references.

"If anyone had asked his (Cho's) roommates whether he ought to be sold a gun, they would have said no," said Paul Helmke, president of the Brady Center to Prevent Gun Violence. "Why not have some sort of reference check?"

Dennis Chastain, an employee of Roanoke Firearms, which sold Cho the Glock 19 pistol he used in his rampage Monday, said he "wouldn't sell" a gun to someone if he knew he had voluntarily received psychiatric treatment.

Cho purchased another handgun on Feb. 9. It was bought from an out-of-state dealer and the paperwork was processed at a pawnshop in Blacksburg, near the Virginia Tech campus. Joe Dowdy, who owns JND Pawn, said he got state police approval to authorize Cho to take the gun.

"I've turned people down before, but there's no way of knowing a buyer's psychological history," Dowdy said. "That's why we call state police."

—Thomas Frank and Chris Colston

CHAPTER FOUR

Are All Firearms Created Equal?

ON APRIL 4, 2009, A PAIR OF PITTSBURGH, Pennsylvania, police officers responded to a call from a mother who wanted her adult son removed from the home. The police didn't know that they were headed for an armed conflict with a disturbed young man.

The man was Richard Poplawski, aged twenty-two. Poplawski had been discharged from the U.S. Marine Corps for attacking his drill sergeant. He was unemployed. He had a history of violent interactions, and he regularly visited white supremacist websites. He was also a gun enthusiast. He was a regular customer at a local gun store, where he bought high-powered semi-automatic weapons and ammunition.

On that fateful night in April 2009, Poplawski got into an argument with his mother. She called the police. Poplawski rushed to his cache of weapons, strapped on a bulletproof vest, slung a semiautomatic AK-47 rifle over his shoulder, and lay in wait.

Left: Pittsburgh police officers investigate the scene outside the home of Richard Poplawski and his mother after he shot three officers there.

The AK-47

It's almost impossible to talk about assault weapons without mentioning the AK-47. This automatic rifle is one of the most famous guns in history. It has served as the model for countless other automatic and semiautomatic weapons.

Russian military officer Mikhail Kalashnikov developed the AK-47 in the 1940s, finally perfecting it in 1947. Its name stands for *Avtomat Kalashnikova 47* (Kalashnikov Automatic Rifle, 1947 model). Over time, the AK-47 proved to be a highly reliable and durable weapon. More than six decades after its release, armies, citizens, and terrorist groups around the world still use the AK-47.

Many countries, including the United States, prohibit private citizens from using automatic weapons. Many assault weapons laws ban the AK-47 and its derivatives (spin-offs) by name. So gun manufacturers have altered AK-47 derivatives to make them into semiautomatic weapons. Semiautomatic versions of the AK-47 make up a large portion of the assault weapons whose legality is so hotly debated.

Above: Mikhail Kalashnikov holds an early model of the AK-47 rifle, which he developed, during an anniversary ceremony in 2007.

When the police arrived, Poplawski opened fire. He shot and killed officer Paul Sciullo inside the house. Then Poplawski shot officer Stephen Mayhle, knocking him down just outside the house. Poplawski stepped over Mayhle and calmly fired several more shots into him. Off-duty officer Eric Kelly, who lived nearby and was just arriving home, heard about the incident on his radio. He headed over. Poplawski shot Kelly as soon as he arrived. Kelly later died of his wounds.

Poplawski continued to fight even after a heavily armed SWAT team arrived. (The acronym SWAT stands for "special weapons and tactics.") He held off the SWAT team for more than four hours. During that time, he wounded two more officers. "It sounded like an actual war zone," said neighbor Georgia Marciniak. "It was absolutely scary."

Eventually Poplawski gave up and surrendered. Police led him from the scene in handcuffs.

The event left the community reeling. No one could understand why Poplawski had done what he did. But there was no denying that his easy access to powerful weaponry had played a big part in the bloodshed. City councilman Doug Shields summarized the tragedy, "Someone with an AK-47 today was angry enough to use it."

THE ARMS WE BEAR

When the founders wrote the Second Amendment, gun technology was much different than in modern times. Guns were slow-loading and cumbersome. Their accuracy and range were poor. Craftsmanship and maintenance made one gun superior to another.

The founders could not have envisioned modern gun technology such as automatic weapons, rocket-propelled grenades, and sawed-off shotguns. They didn't need to distinguish which arms people could keep and bear because in the young United States, the available weapons differed little. Some argue that in this respect, the Second Amendment is badly outdated.

This change in technology poses a difficult challenge for twenty-first century lawmakers. They must decide: Does the Second Amendment guarantee the right to own any and all arms? Or can it still give everyone the right to gun ownership while still restricting which weapons are allowed?

The U.S. judicial system first grappled with this issue in 1939. Two men had been arrested for carrying an unregistered shotgun with a barrel of less than 18 inches (46 centimeters) from one state to another—a violation of the National Firearms Act of 1934. The men argued that this law violated their Second Amendment rights. Their case, called *United States v. Miller*, rose to the Supreme Court.

The high court's justices determined that the National Firearms Act of 1934 did not violate the Second Amendment. Explaining the Court's decision, Justice James McReynolds wrote, "In the absence of any evidence tending to show that possession or use of a 'shotgun having a barrel of less than eighteen inches in length' at this time has some reasonable relationship to the preservation or efficiency of a well regulated militia, we cannot say that the Second Amendment guarantees the right to keep and bear such an instrument. Certainly it is not within judicial notice that this weapon is any part of the ordinary military equipment or that its use could contribute to the common defense." In short, the Court said that the government did have the right to limit the types of firearms citizens could own.

United States v. Miller leaves an awful lot of room for interpretation, however. This ruling says that the government can dictate which weapons the Second Amendment protects. But people still argue about whether the government should do so. If the answer is yes, which arms are in—and which are out? Modern weaponry is as varied as it is advanced.

ASSAULT WEAPONS

Most privately owned guns in the United States serve one or

more of three purposes: self-defense, sport shooting, or hunting. Contrary to some claims, the U.S. government has never shown interest in denying law-abiding citizens guns for these purposes. Waiting periods and background checks don't stop responsible people from owning weapons. These deterrents are merely hurdles over which would-be gun owners must jump.

The government has, however, shown interest in banning weapons that go beyond gun owners' basic needs. Ultra-long-range sniper rifles, automatic and semiautomatic weapons, high-caliber weapons, and armor-piercing ammunition are better suited for military purposes than for self-defense, sport shooting, or hunting. Should U.S. law keep such powerful weapons away from ordinary citizens?

Some believe that it should. They think that such weaponry serves no purpose outside military settings. It can only lead to unnecessary harm.

Others think that if the Second Amendment guarantees the right to bear arms, it guarantees the right to bear all arms. They believe lawmakers should not pick and choose which arms are available.

Above: This high-powered sniper rifle is one assault weapon that gun-control advocates would like to ban for civilian use.

Assault weapons: A primer

Legal definition

A weapon that can accept a magazine, or bullet chamber, that can easily be removed. It has at least two "assault" features, such as a flash suppressor (which suppresses the light when the weapon is fired) or a protruding pistol grip (which allows it to be held like a pistol).

Intratec TEC-9/DC-9
Made in the USA. Semiautomatic version of an automatic pistol. Can handle magazines with up to 50 rounds.

Well-known types

Colt AR-15
Made in the USA. Semiautomatic version of the M-16 military rifle. Holds 9 rounds standard, more with "high-capacity" magazines. Has a pistol grip and flash suppressor.

Streetsweeper
U.S.-made version of the Striker-12 shotgun that is made in South Africa. Police often have cited its use among gangs. Holds 12 rounds in a rotating chamber.

Beretta AR-70
Made in Italy. Assault rifle that initially was used by Italian special forces. Can fire 650 rounds per minute; its magazine can hold 30 rounds. Comes with pistol grips.

Note: Firearms not to scale.

Norinco MAK-90
Made in China. Semiautomatic version of the AK-47. Has a 30-round magazine but can handle larger magazines.

Criminals using guns

A Justice Department survey of federal and state inmates in 1997 said that fewer than 2% had used assault weapons in their crimes, many of which took place before the ban in 1994. The National Rifle Association says this suggests lifting the ban will have a minor impact on criminals' use of such weapons. Citing the same study, gun-control advocates note that only 20% of criminals used any gun and say that a disproportionate percentage of those criminals — 6.8% in state cases; 9.3% in federal cases — used semiautomatic weapons. They say that suggests lifting the ban will lead more criminals to use them.

Assault weapons in high-profile slayings

▶ Littleton, Colo., 1999: Columbine High School students Dylan Klebold and Eric Harris used an Intratec TEC-9, among other weapons, to carry out a rampage at the school that killed 13 people.
▶ McLean, Va., 1993: Mir Aimal Kasi, a Pakistani national, killed two CIA employees and injured three others outside the agency's headquarters. He used an AK-47 made in China. Kasi was executed in November 2002.

Sources: Reporting by Melanie Eversley, USA TODAY; Brady Campaign to Prevent Gun Violence; Physicians for Social Responsibility; www.AWBanSunset.com; Modern Firearms and Ammunition; National Rifle Association; North American Special Operations Group; State of California Office of the Attorney General; The Arms Site; USA TODAY research; and wire reports

By Karl Gelles, USA TODAY, 2004

Lawmakers must figure out whether to ban certain weapons. And if they decide to do so, they must also figure out where to draw the line.

The Federal Assault Weapons Ban (AWB) of 1994 tried to address this issue. Generally speaking, it defined assault weapons as automatic weapons (which were already banned) or semiautomatic ones. A semiautomatic weapon automatically makes new ammunition ready to fire after each pull of the trigger. The AWB banned nineteen specific semiautomatic gun models by name. But the ban left many loopholes. It applied only to guns made after the ban took effect. Gun manufacturers could make minor changes to their weapons to get around the ban. The general consensus—on both sides of the gun-control debate—was that the AWB had little effect on the flow of assault weapons.

The AWB expired in 2004. A ten-year extension of the AWB was crushed in the U.S. Senate by a vote of 90–8. The issue of a new assault weapons ban has come up many times since 2004. Opponents of a new ban argue that since the first ban didn't work, there's no

❝These [assault weapons] are not weapons that people use for hunting, and, in fact, if you use one of these weapons for hunting, you couldn't eat the animal because the animal wouldn't exist anymore. . . . Who uses these weapons? Drug dealers, terrorists, the scum of our society.❞

—U.S. REPRESENTATIVE PETER DEUTSCH OF FLORIDA, 1996

> ❝ **There's not a dime's worth of difference between the guns you want to ban and you don't want to ban. You're going to ban these semi-autos, and then it's going to be handguns, and then it's going to be pump shotguns.** ❞

—**WAYNE LAPIERRE,** EXECUTIVE VICE PRESIDENT OF THE NRA, 2009

reason to believe another one will. Meanwhile, supporters of a new ban blame the NRA and other pro-gun groups for the AWB's failure. They claim that the groups lobbied Congress so hard against the original bill that only a weak, ineffective law could pass. Without gun-lobby interference, supporters say, a stronger bill could get the job done.

HANDGUNS

Handguns are another battleground in the gun-control debate. Unlike long-barreled rifles and shotguns, handguns aren't useful for hunters. Because a handgun has a short barrel, it doesn't have the long-range accuracy needed for hunting. Likewise, sport shooters rarely use handguns. A handgun drawn outside a shooting range is probably going to be aimed at a human being.

Some people see handguns as a problem because they're concealable and easy to operate. A person doesn't need much gun knowledge or skill to wield a handgun effectively. Almost anybody, including a child, can pick up and use a handgun—unlike a rifle, which requires a certain level of strength and competence. The vast majority of shooting accidents and crimes involve handguns. For these reasons, some people want to ban handguns or at least control them more tightly.

Others see the size and simplicity of handguns in a positive light. They argue that handguns are vital self-defense tools, especially for smaller or weaker users who have difficulty handling larger guns. Handguns serve as equalizers. With a handgun, anyone can defend him- or herself—even against an accomplished criminal. Gun-rights supporters say that this is the very reason the founders protected Americans' right to keep and bear arms.

Below: A group of people shoot handguns at an outdoor range. Many people see handguns as a way for ordinary citizens to protect themselves from criminals.

Criminals are packing more heat

From the Pages of
USA TODAY

Criminals increasingly are choosing high-powered firearms such as assault weapons, a new survey of 166 U.S. police agencies shows.

Nearly 40% of the departments reported an uptick in the use of assault weapons, according to the Police Executive Research Forum, a law enforcement think tank. In addition, half reported increases in the use of 9mm, .40-caliber and 10mm handguns in crimes—among the same types of weapons that police use. The survey offers one of the broadest indications of officers' concerns about the armed threat from criminals involved in murder, assault and other weapons-related offenses.

Among problems cited by police officials in interviews about the survey:

- Chicago. Seizures of assault weapons are up, from 264 in 2008 to 313 in 2009. Overall, 7,785 weapons were recovered this year, up from 6,963 in 2008. Chicago Police Superintendent Jody Weis says there is evidence that more weapons are being used per shooting and more shots are being fired.
- Milwaukee. Semiautomatic 9mm and .40-caliber handguns were used in the non-fatal shootings of six city police officers over a 21-month period, ending Sept. 30. "The quality of weapons (used by criminals) has changed dramatically in the past decade," Police Chief Edward Flynn says.
- Louisville. Weapons-related arrests are on pace to rise in 2009 for the second consecutive year. "We're seeing higher-caliber weapons, a lot more automatic weapons," Police Chief Robert White says. "The criminals know you don't take a bow-and-arrow to a gunfight."

National Rifle Association spokesman Andrew Arulanandam says officers' concerns are largely misplaced: "The real issue is the high-caliber criminal, not the high-caliber firearms." He says repeat offenders are overwhelming the system and could increase as states send fewer to prison to cut costs.

Paul Helmke, president of the Brady Campaign to Prevent Gun Violence, says the high-powered weapons endanger officers. If police say there's a problem, "public officials should be listening."

—Kevin Johnson

CONTROLLING AMMUNITION

The gun-control debate isn't always about guns. Sometimes it's about ammunition. Most bullets go straight through a target. But specialty ammo behaves differently.

Several kinds of specialty ammunition exist. Armor-piercing ammunition is made with ultrahard metal such as tungsten, steel, brass, bronze, and iron. Incendiary ammo contains chemicals that ignite (catch fire) on impact. Fragmentation ammo shatters on impact, launching many deadly shards of metal. Exploding bullets contain chemicals that create small explosions on impact. Large-caliber ammunition refers to extra-large bullets and other large projectiles fired from guns. High-capacity magazines are ammo-feeding devices that hold large amounts of ammo.

Many Americans support controls on specialty ammunition. Congress has passed laws that address this issue. For example, the Gun Control Act of 1968 bans certain types of armor-piercing ammunition.

Those who support the ban argue that such ammo endangers police and other law enforcement officers. The AWB of 1994 banned high-capacity magazines on the premise that no civilian needs more than a few shots for self-defense. Restrictions on other types of ammunition vary by state.

Opponents to restrictions on specialty ammunition say that it's not the government's place to decide how a civilian defends him- or herself. They also point out that ammo restrictions don't stop criminals from using illegal ammunition.

HEAVY ARTILLERY

Most of the U.S. debate over the right to keep and bear arms focuses on guns. But what about other weapons? Should the Second Amendment cover heavy artillery such as rocket launchers, grenade launchers, high explosives, and missiles? The U.S. government keeps these weapons away from common citizens. But should it? The debate here is similar to the debate over assault weapons. It

Above: Heavy artillery, such as this grenade launcher, are restricted by the U.S. government. But some people believe the Second Amendment guarantees citizen access to all weapons, including heavy artillery.

seeks to answer the same question: how far do Second Amendment rights extend?

Most Americans agree that common citizens have no need for heavy artillery. Most people believe that such weapons are appropriate only for military use, not for individual self-defense, target practice, and certainly not for hunting. Using a rocket launcher to repel an intruder, bag a deer, or hone one's marksmanship would be overkill.

But not everyone agrees with this view. Some people argue that the Second Amendment is meant to ensure that private citizens have the weaponry they need to overthrow an invading force or a tyrant at home.

Hunting rifles and handguns wouldn't do the job, they say. Neither would assault weapons. An invading army, for example, would have armored vehicles, heavy machine guns, and high explosives. Private citizens wouldn't stand a chance unless they were similarly armed.

The debate over heavy artillery is mostly theoretical (about ideas, rather than actions). A citizen militia armed with such weapons is not realistic. The cost alone is prohibitively high. Only the wealthy could ever afford one such weapon—much less an arsenal of them.

CHAPTER FIVE

Measures of Control

MINNESOTA STATE REPRESENTATIVE MICHAEL Paymar called a press conference to discuss his proposal for a new state law. This law would require background checks for firearms purchases made at gun shows. Paymar wanted to make an impression.

That's where retired sheriff's deputy Jerry Dhennin came in. Dhennin, who described himself as a "gun nut," entered the press conference with a semiautomatic Ruger Mini-14 assault rifle strapped over his shoulder. Dhennin showed off the gun. He said he'd purchased it from a vendor at a gun show by doing nothing more than flashing a driver's license. Dhennin then produced a 9mm semiautomatic pistol, also purchased with no questions asked.

"There's no reason to have that kind of firepower that I know of except maybe for law enforcement and the military," Dhennin explained. "But yet I was able to buy this at a gun show, no questions asked, except that I was required to show a driver's license by Minnesota law."

Left: Jerry Dhennin holds an assault rifle as he testifies before a Minnesota House of Representatives committee in March 2010. Dhennin urgest the Minnesota legislature to pass a law making it more difficult to buy guns at gun shows.

"There's something very wrong with this picture," Dhennin later added.

Paymar explained his proposal. "We can save lives and keep some guns out of the streets in Minnesota if we plug these loopholes by trying to ensure that dangerous people don't possess dangerous weapons," he said.

Gun-rights activists disagreed with Paymar. They argued that few guns used in crime come from gun shows and that no evidence demonstrates that gun-show sales significantly affect crime rates. Furthermore, they believe that making firearms easy to purchase results in a better armed citizenry, which in turn deters crime. "This bill has no effect on criminals at all," said Joe Olson of the Gun Owners Civil Rights Alliance. "It's not intended to have an effect on criminals. It's only intended to make gun ownership and gun possession a bigger hassle."

LICENSING AND REGISTRATION

Every teenager in every U.S. state knows that a license is needed to drive a car. Motor vehicles are large, powerful, and potentially dangerous machines. To drive one, a person must first demonstrate the ability to operate it safely.

A gun license grants a user the right to own and use a firearm. Registration is the act of registering each gun with a state or local agency. A permit grants a gun owner the right to carry the firearm in public. No federal law requires gun licensing, registration, or permits. Gun-licensing laws vary by state. Some states require full licensing and registration of all firearms, while other states require only a permit to carry and conceal a weapon.

Some gun-control supporters believe that federal guidelines for licensing and registration are needed. They argue that gun use should follow the same standard as driving. They contend that guns are highly dangerous weapons. Misuse can endanger a user and everyone else nearby. The federal government has a responsibility, therefore,

Above: The Massachusetts secretary of public safety holds up new and old state firearms licenses in 2004.

to make sure gun owners know how to handle their guns safely and responsibly. Just as a driver's test ensures basic competence among licensed drivers, so would gun licensing among gun owners. Furthermore, registration of guns helps law enforcement organizations track guns used in crime. Registration lists track gun owners and the guns they own, providing a valuable database in criminal investigations.

Gun-rights supporters strongly oppose federally mandated (required) licensing or registration. They see both as dangerous steps toward revoking Second Amendment rights.

Microstamping

Matching a bullet to the gun that fired it is an important and difficult job for law enforcement agents conducting a criminal investigation. Some people advocate using a technology called microstamping to give law enforcement a hand.

Firearm microstamping, also called ballistic imprinting and ballistic engraving, gives each gun a unique "fingerprint." A microstamped gun has a small laser-engraved design on its firing pin. This microstamp leaves a unique mark on the casing of fired ammunition. This mark tells police exactly which gun fired the bullet. Police can then check sales and registration records to get a lead on the case.

Above: This image shows a casing being ejected from a handgun as it is fired. Microstamping imprints each casing with a unique identifier as the gun is fired. This identifier helps law enforcement track the owner of the gun.

They say that with mandated licensing or registration, a right guaranteed by the Constitution becomes a privilege granted by the government. The Second Amendment grants all Americans the right to keep and bear arms—not just the Americans that the state deems responsible enough to do so or the Americans who are willing to register their firearms. Gun-rights supporters also argue that a tyrannical government could use licensing or registration lists to disarm a population. Such a government could use such lists to identify gun owners and seize their weapons, leaving the citizenry defenseless.

Federal laws do address the licensing of firearms dealers. The Gun Control Act of 1968 and the Firearm Owners' Protection Act of 1986 require certain gun and ammunition sellers to obtain a Federal Firearms License (FFL). Licensed dealers must submit buyers' names for background checks. However, not everyone selling guns has to have an FFL. The requirement applies only to sellers who meet certain standards, such as those who sell firearms at retail or wholesale prices or who make their primary living dealing in firearms. Individual collectors who sell their firearms do not have to obtain a license and do not have to do background checks. Some people think this loophole needs to be closed. Why should some dealers have to be licensed, but not others? For gun-control advocates, the solution is to force every firearms seller to be licensed. Meanwhile, some gun-rights supporters suggest abandoning the flawed federal licensing system altogether.

BACKGROUND CHECKS

Background checks are another way to control the flow of guns in the United States. The Brady Handgun Violence Prevention Act of 1993 mandates such checks. At first background checks took several days. Buyers had to wait five days between applying for a gun purchase and completing the purchase.

In November 1998, the FBI unveiled the National Instant

States bolster FBI gun database

From the Pages of USA TODAY

More states are turning over records to a federal database of mentally ill people barred from owning guns, nearly tripling the number in the system since the [2007] massacre at Virginia Tech last spring, the FBI says.

The tragedy spurred states to revisit their policies regarding the database. The FBI's National Instant Criminal Background Check System (NICS), which federally licensed gun dealers must consult before selling a gun, has about 402,000 records from 32 states of people declared mentally ill by a court, FBI records show. On April 1, 2007, two weeks before the Virginia Tech shooting, the database had 165,778 records from 22 states. The federal government cannot force states to transmit their records.

Illinois is one of the states that began sending mental-health records to the federal database after the Virginia Tech shooting. Steven Kazmierczak, the gunman who last week killed five students at Northern Illinois University before turning the gun on himself, was not in the database and purchased his guns legally, says Stephen Fischer, a spokesman for the FBI Criminal Justice Information Services Division.

States send records only after a court has committed individuals for involuntary psychiatric treatment or found them to be dangerous to themselves or others. Kazmierczak, 27, had been seeing a psychiatrist in the months before the rampage, his girlfriend, Jessica Baty, told CNN.

Criminal Background Check System (NICS). Using this electronic system, federally licensed gun dealers can perform an instant background check on anyone trying to purchase a firearm. The dealer completes a document called a Firearms Transaction Record. It includes information about the buyer and the gun. The dealer submits this document to NICS, which informs the dealer of the buyer's status within minutes. The dealer can get one of three responses:

1. Proceed: This response allows the dealer to complete the transaction according to applicable state laws.

Even with the additional records, the mental-health database is far from complete. The mental illness section of the database has the fewest records of the three components the FBI checks when federally licensed firearms dealers call for background information, says Bobby Hamil, chief of the NICS section. The others show warrants and sexual-offender registries as well as criminal histories.

"We're missing 80 to 90% of the mentally ill. . . . That's scary," says Paul Helmke, president of the Brady Campaign to Prevent Gun Violence, a gun-control advocacy group. Helmke says the missing records stem from "the inertia [slowness] of bureaucracy" rather than strong ideological [philosophical] opposition.

The Brady Campaign estimates the database should have at least 2 million records. Of the 32 states that contribute, 16 sent 50 records or fewer. Seven have contributed just one record, Fischer says.

The bulk of the records come from three states: California, Virginia and Michigan, which contribute about 368,000 of the 402,000 records, FBI records show. The big boost in the database came in October, when California added 200,000 records to the system.

Hamil says he expects that a new law President [George W.] Bush signed in January will prod even more states into sending records. It gives states grants to pay for collecting the information and transmitting it to the federal database. States that don't participate could lose federal money for law enforcement. "It's going to be a real incentive for the states," he says. "Clearly, we're going to see more records coming."

—Donna Leinwand

2. Denied: This response means that the background check turned up information—usually a criminal record—that prevents the buyer from legally owning a firearm.

3. Delayed: This response means that the background check turned up information that might prevent the buyer from legally owning a firearm, but the information is incomplete and requires further investigation. NICS officials have three days to contact the dealer with an approval or a denial. If the dealer does not hear from NICS officials within three days, the dealer can complete the sale.

> ❝ **We require background checks for teachers, and for coaches and for some people in certain jobs. Why then, would you not require them for dangerous people who buy guns?** ❞

—**JOAN PETERSON,** PRESIDENT OF THE MINNESOTA MILLION MOM
CHAPTERS OF THE BRADY CAMPAIGN TO PREVENT GUN VIOLENCE, 2010

Since NICS began, it has stopped more than seven hundred thousand gun sales to people who couldn't legally buy a gun. Supporters say this number shows that background checks slow the flow of guns to people who shouldn't have guns.

Meanwhile, opponents of background checks argue that they're only partly effective. They don't prevent straw purchase—a transaction in which one person buys a firearm on another person's behalf—and they don't apply to transactions between individuals. Sometimes background checks prevent the wrong people from buying firearms. A person who has the same name as a convicted felon, for example,

may encounter difficulties. The information in the NICS database is entered manually. If someone enters data incorrectly, a dangerous criminal may slip through the cracks or a dealer may wrongly deny a law-abiding citizen's gun purchase. Others argue that background checks are an invasion of privacy. On the whole, opponents believe that the background-check system is badly flawed and that its drawbacks outweigh its benefits.

GUN SHOWS

Gun shows are a big business in the United States. Gun manufacturers, dealers, and enthusiasts gather at gun shows to display, buy, sell, trade, and discuss firearms of all kinds. Manufacturers often use these events to show off new models and new features.

But gun shows are a source of controversy too. Many Americans are concerned about how guns are bought and sold at shows. Federal Firearms Licensees must always run background checks on buyers, even at gun shows. But only some of the vendors at gun shows are FFLs. Shows also host many informal, unlicensed vendors. In many states, unlicensed vendors can buy and sell guns without performing background checks.

Gun-control activists argue that this is an unacceptable loophole in gun law. Americans have invested a great deal of time and effort in crafting laws meant to keep guns out of the wrong hands. Many gun-control laws are useless if anyone can walk into a gun show and walk out with a gun.

> ❝The [background check] system isn't working because states have failed to do an adequate job of getting records of people who've been convicted of crimes or people who have been institutionalized or people who have committed domestic violence crimes— getting those records onto a computer tape that can be accessed when a background check is put through for gun buyers. ❞

—**JIM KESSLER,** AMERICANS FOR GUN SAFETY, 2002

Fans of gun show display dismay at sales ban

From the Pages of
USA TODAY

LOS ANGELES—To its promoters and fans, the Great Western Gun Show is only peripherally [a little bit] about guns.

Most visitors are so solidly middle class that the U.S. Marines, the Los Angeles Police Department and the county Sheriff's Department all set up recruiting booths. It can sometimes feel like a costume party, where men come dressed in Civil War uniforms or whole families attend in camouflage.

Of the 5,300 display tables that stretch for eight miles [13 kilometers], fewer than 10% hold modern guns. The rest display old war medals, gun accessories such as straps and scopes, canteens and beef jerky.

But what's a gun show without guns for sale?

That is what's the country's largest gun show is facing at its big fall event this October because of a law approved Tuesday, on a 3-2 vote, by the Los Angeles County Board of Supervisors. The ordinance [law], effective just one month before the Great Western Gun Show opens at the county fairgrounds in Pomona, outlaws all gun sales on county property.

It doesn't exclude gun shows from being staged at the fairgrounds, where the Great Western show has operated for 22 years. Vendors can still exhibit their weapons. They just can't put them up for sale or even make arrangements to sell them at a later date.

The prohibition produced much harrumphing among dozens of gun show aficionados [experts] who attended the debate. They said that a gun show where they couldn't buy guns would be no more than a trip around a museum.

The show's promoters are vowing to go to court to overturn the ban. Contracts already have been signed for shows in October and December, two of the four held annually.

"Fewer people will come to the show," predicted Chad Segar, the show's manager.

The debate over gun shows is part of a growing assault on firearms in California.

Above: A gun-show attendee visits with a dealer at the Great Western Gun Show in Los Angeles, California, in 1999. Due to a change in local gun laws, the Great Western Gun Show moved to Las Vegas, Nevada, the next year.

Politicians have been emboldened to press for stricter gun legislation by the arrests of vendors who sold illegal weapons to undercover agents at earlier shows, as well as by tragedy. On Aug. 10, a gunman with a history of mental illness wounded five people at a Jewish community center here, then killed a Filipino-American letter carrier.

Last month, the state Legislature enacted a ban on assault weapons and junk handguns. Other handgun purchases are now limited to one a month. Soon, guns must be sold in California with child-safety locks. Now, gun shows are facing increased scrutiny.

"Gun shows are not good or bad," said Los Angeles County Sheriff Lee Baca, who testified in support of the gun-sale ban. "But what we're dealing with is a small portion of vendors who sell illegal weapons. Assault weapons, military weapons, junk guns—all this stuff has passed through the hands of vendors at gun shows."

Dozens of speakers, however, argued that a ban would penalize visitors who regard gun shows as entertainment.

"I'm not a criminal," said Alwyn Crow, who works in food service at UCLA and has attended the Great Western show for years. "You'll prevent law-abiding citizens from the peaceful assembly and purchase of a legal product from licensed dealers. If you put as much fervor into the capture and prosecution of criminals that you do to the harassment of people who attend gun shows, Los Angeles would be a much better place to live."

—Carol Morello

Straw Purchase

Even background checks can't always keep the guns out of the wrong hands. Gun shows have, fairly or not, become notorious for a practice called a straw purchase. These illegal gun purchases happen when someone is not able to buy a gun legally. Perhaps the individual is too young or has a disqualifying criminal record. So the person has someone else make the purchase on his or her behalf.

People who buy guns from licensed dealers must confirm in writing that they are purchasing the guns for themselves. But some people don't take this requirement seriously.

Gun enthusiasts counter that gun shows are an important part of gun culture in the United States. The shows offer gun owners a sense of community and serve as an educational tool. Small vendors cannot be expected to do background checks, they claim. Having to do so would grind their business to an effective halt. Some don't think gun shows are a significant source of guns used in crime. Others simply don't think that the irresponsible actions of a few criminals should ruin the experience for all the law-abiding citizens who enjoy the shows.

Some states have passed laws to close the gun-show loophole. In 2009 members of the U.S. Congress proposed two laws to address it at a federal level. The bills, called the Gun Show Loophole Closing Act of 2009 and the Gun Show Background Check Act of 2009, got strong support from the Brady Campaign to Prevent Gun Violence and opposition from the NRA and other gun-rights groups. The NRA claimed that both bills were little more than veiled attempts to shut down the gun-show industry. By January 2011, neither bill had come to a vote.

Above: Two off-duty Los Angeles sheriff deputies attend a gun show in Las Vegas, Nevada, in 2011. Many people attend gun shows each year. Debate rages over unrestricted gun sales at gun shows.

CONCEALED CARRY

It's one thing to own a gun. The Second Amendment protects that right. But do citizens have the right to carry guns in public? And if so, do they have the right to conceal their weapons?

In most U.S. states, people who wish to carry concealed firearms must have permits to do so. Permit requirements vary by state. They may include residency, age, fingerprinting, passing a background check, attending a gun-safety class, and paying a fee. All U.S. states fall into four basic categories regarding permits to conceal and carry a weapon in public.

1. Unrestricted: Unrestricted states do not require permits to carry concealed guns.
2. Shall Issue: A Shall-Issue state issues concealed carry permits to all individuals who meet the permit's requirements.

3. May Issue: A May-Issue state gives local authorities the power to decide which qualified applicants will receive permits. Applicants may have to provide some reason for needing to carry and conceal weapons.
4. No Issue: No-Issue states do not allow private citizens to carry concealed handguns.

What are the pros and cons of letting private citizens carry concealed weapons? Should the U.S. government restrict concealed carry rights? How much?

Some gun-control advocates think concealed carry laws need to be stricter. They argue that citizens walking around with loaded guns tucked in their clothing are a danger to everyone. The case of professional football player Plaxico Burress illustrates this argument. In 2008 Burress went to a New York City nightclub with a handgun tucked in the waistband of his pants. Burress did not have a concealed carry permit. He claimed that he carried the gun because he feared being attacked. When Burress felt the handgun slipping down the leg of his pants, he grabbed for the gun and accidentally pressed the trigger. The bullet hit his right leg. Burress was not seriously wounded. But his accident highlighted the danger of citizens carrying concealed weapons—especially without permits.

Above: Plaxico Burress, a professional football player, is a famous example of someone who accidentally shot himself when concealing a handgun.

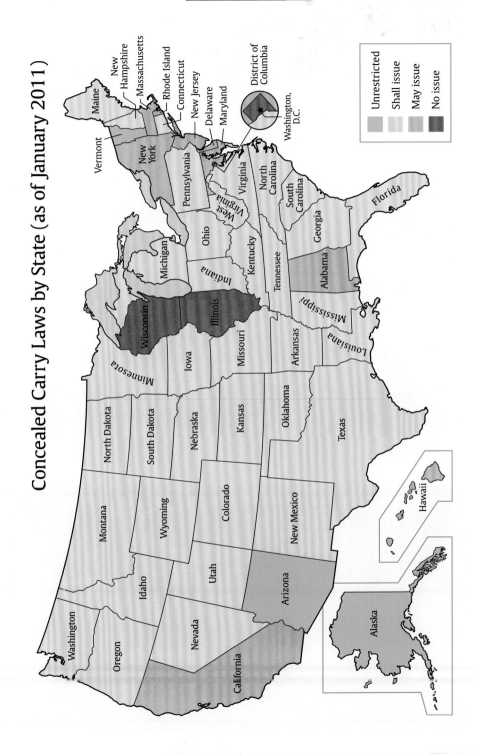

Concealed Carry Laws by State (as of January 2011)

Maine
New Hampshire
Massachusetts
Rhode Island
Connecticut
New Jersey
Delaware
Maryland
District of Columbia
Washington, D.C.

Unrestricted
Shall issue
May issue
No issue

Vermont
New York
Pennsylvania
West Virginia
Virginia
North Carolina
South Carolina
Florida
Michigan
Ohio
Indiana
Kentucky
Tennessee
Georgia
Alabama
Mississippi
Wisconsin
Illinois
Iowa
Missouri
Arkansas
Louisiana
Minnesota
North Dakota
South Dakota
Nebraska
Kansas
Oklahoma
Texas
Montana
Wyoming
Colorado
New Mexico
Washington
Idaho
Utah
Arizona
Oregon
Nevada
California

Hawaii
Alaska

The bullet could have struck an innocent bystander. Burress was later found guilty of illegally possessing weapons and of reckless endangerment. A court sentenced him to two years in prison.

Meanwhile, many gun-rights supporters think concealed carry restrictions go too far. The threat of an armed citizen is a powerful crime deterrent, they say. Criminals are likely to carry weapons regardless of whether they have permits. So permit restrictions apply only to law-abiding citizens. Gun-rights supporters argue that this leaves everyone less safe. When criminals know that citizens are unlikely to be carrying weapons, they have less fear of carrying out their crimes.

GUN-FREE ZONES

Even when a person has legal permission to carry a gun, he or she can't do so everywhere. In 1990 the U.S. Congress passed the Gun-Free School Zones Act. This law declared schools and the areas around them to be

Above: Most schools post signs declaring their grounds gun-free. This school is in Phoenix, Arizona.

gun-free zones. The U.S. Supreme Court struck it down as unconstitutional in 1995, but Congress quickly replaced it with the Gun-Free School Zones Act of 1995. This law is a revised version of the 1990 law. It places strict limitations on where citizens can carry firearms. It forbids any firearms on school grounds (kindergarten through twelfth grade) or in public areas (streets, sidewalks, and so on) within 1,000 feet (305 meters) of a school. States can grant exemptions to individual permit holders.

State and federal laws allow for many other gun-free zones. These include post offices, hospitals, shopping malls, churches, and more. Some states allow individual businesses to prohibit weapons on their property.

Supporters of gun-free zones argue that they protect innocents, especially children. Laws that keep guns away from schools and other vulnerable areas can reduce children's risk of becoming the victims of gun violence.

Opponents argue the opposite. They say that criminals ignore the law, and laws designating gun-free zones are no exception. If a criminal went on a shooting rampage in a gun-free zone, no one would have the firepower needed to stop him or her. Furthermore, opponents argue that gun-free zones are unconstitutional because they strip people of their Second Amendment rights.

GUN BUYBACKS

In recent decades, city leaders across the United States have become worried about the number of guns on the streets, especially among youth. Many cities have started programs to remove some of these guns from circulation. These programs, often called gun buybacks, offer cash (from $25 to $250), gift cards, or other incentives in exchange for each gun. In most programs, anyone can exchange a gun with no questions asked.

Whether buyback programs work is debatable. Supporters point to programs that bring in thousands of guns. One program in Washington, D.C., took more than four thousand guns off the

Above: Members of the Los Angeles Police Department show Mayor Antonio Villaraigosa *(second from right)* handguns collected through the city's gun buyback program in 2009.

By reducing the number of guns in an area, gun buybacks can reduce gun violence.

But do buybacks really reduce gun violence? The U.S. Department of Justice says that guns turned in to buyback programs are the guns least likely to have been used for crime. In short, criminals aren't the ones turning their guns in.

That's irrelevant, according to some buyback supporters. They argue that any gun off the streets is a gun that can't fall into the wrong hands. "That little old lady's gun at the bottom of a closet often finds its way to somebody who's up to no good when her house is burglarized," said Roland Holmgren, spokesperson for the Oakland, California, police department.

street. Someone even turned in two hand grenades. Supporters of gun buybacks say that every gun taken off the street is one gun that cannot be used in an illegal or accidental shooting.

Some buyback skeptics point out that even taking thousands of guns off the streets makes little difference. "It's like trying to drain the Pacific with a bucket," said Alex Tabarrok, research director at Independent Institute, a non-profit think tank. "More guns are going to flow in." Worldwide, gun makers produce about eight million guns per year.

Supporters counter that gun buyback programs don't cost much. They're just one part of a larger puzzle, but every piece matters.

EPILOGUE

An Uncertain Future

A CENTURY AGO, ALMOST NO DEBATE OVER GUN control existed in the United States. Americans simply didn't worry much about gun rights or gun violence. But since then, concern over the issue has grown. Is gun ownership a danger to Americans, or does it keep the nation safe? What role should the government play in determining who can own firearms and which firearms they can own?

With each passing decade, the debate has grown more hostile and the arguments more extreme. Likewise, legislation has grown increasingly abundant—and increasingly complicated. In the 1960s, Americans disagreed over strategies to reduce gun violence while protecting gun rights. But they also worked together toward compromise.

Left: President Barack Obama speaks at the memorial service for the six people who died during the shooting attack on U.S. Representative Gabrielle Giffords of Arizona on January 12, 2011. In March, President Obama wrote an editorial for the *Arizona Daily Star*. In his editorial, the president discussed his views on preventing gun violence while balancing the rights of gun owners.

Since then, the two sides of the issue have drifted further and further apart. In the twenty-first century, gun-control and gun-rights advocates cannot seem to find common ground upon which to build compromise. Each side has dug in its heels and refuses to budge. As a result, the issue has become a political football—a matter that's continually debated but never resolved. The aftermath of the 2011 assassination attempt on Gabrielle Giffords illustrated this problem. Instead of uniting in tragedy, both sides of the debate went on the attack. Neither side showed much interest in compromise. For many Americans, the tragedy became just another reason to argue.

Above: Gun owners rally at the state capitol in Springfield, Illinois, on March 11, 2009. The demonstrators seek new laws that would allow them to carry concealed weapons.

USA TODAY Snapshots®

Should gun laws be more strict?

Percentage who said yes:

1990
78%

2000
62%

2009
44%

Source:
Gallup survey of 1,013
adults Oct. 1–4

By Anne R. Carey and Sam Ward, USA TODAY, 2009

In truth, most Americans fall somewhere between the two extremes. Most Americans treasure the liberties guaranteed by the Bill of Rights. Freedom of speech, freedom of religion, and the freedom to keep and bear arms are key elements of the United States' greatness, they say. At the same time, polls reveal that most Americans believe some level of gun control is necessary. News programs and newspapers constantly deliver stories about gun violence in the United States. Americans want their government to help ensure their safety. They simply differ on the best way for the government to do so.

The proper balance between gun control and gun rights will probably remain an issue of public debate well into the twenty-first century. As increasingly powerful weapons become more affordable and more available, lawmakers will face difficult decisions on how to protect Americans' safety and their rights simultaneously.

TIMELINE

1100s   Debate rages in Europe over a deadly new weapon, the crossbow.

1300s   People develop modern firearms such as cannons and guns in both Europe and China.

1400s   Guns become common but remain clumsy.

1500s   Gun design starts advancing rapidly. European settlers begin moving to North America, establishing a culture of guns there.

1594   Queen Elizabeth I of England bans the wheel-lock pistol.

1700s   Thirteen British colonies dominate the eastern seaboard of North America. The colonies grow self-sufficient and resentful of British interference.

1775   The American Revolution begins.

1776   The thirteen colonies declare independence from Great Britain and form the United States of America.

1783   The American Revolution ends.

1787   Representatives of the young United States sign its Constitution.

1791   U.S. lawmakers add the Bill of Rights to the Constitution. This document includes the Second Amendment, which grants Americans the right to keep and bear arms.

1871   William Church and George Wingate form the National Rifle Association.

1873   An election dispute erupts in Louisiana, leading to the U.S. Supreme Court case *United States v. Cruikshank*. The case determines that the Second Amendment applies only to the federal government, not to individuals or groups.

1876   A crowd of armed citizens in Northfield, Minnesota, foil a bank robbery by the Jesse James gang.

1927 To address the growing problem of organized crime, Congress passes the Mailing of Firearms Act, which outlaws the shipping of concealable handguns by U.S. mail.

1934 Congress passes the National Firearms Act, which taxes the sales of short-barreled rifles and shotguns, automatic weapons, silencers, and explosive devices. The law requires registration for these weapons. The law does not include handguns, thanks to a massive NRA letter-writing campaign.

1938 Congress passes the Federal Firearms Act, which bans the sale of firearms to convicted felons and fugitives. It also bars unlicensed dealers from selling guns across state lines.

1939 In *United States v. Miller*, the U.S. Supreme Court rules that the government has the right to limit the types of firearms citizens may own.

1947 Mikhail Kalashnikov perfects the AK-47.

1963 Lee Harvey Oswald assassinates President John F. Kennedy using a cheap imported gun ordered through the NRA magazine the *American Rifleman*. The assassination reignites the gun-control debate.

1968 In response to a series of assassinations and violet riots, Congress passes the Gun Control Act, the nation's first comprehensive gun-control legislation. This law establishes the Bureau of Alcohol, Tobacco and Firearms (ATF).

1970s The NRA evolves into a large, powerful organization strongly opposed to all gun control.

1981 An assassination attempt on President Ronald Reagan seriously injures his press secretary, James Brady. The Bradys form the Brady Campaign to Prevent Gun Violence.

1986 Congress passes the Firearm Owners' Protection Act, scaling back the Gun Control Act of 1968.

1990   Congress passes the Gun-Free School Zones Act.

1993   Congress passes the Brady Handgun Violence Prevention Act, mandating background checks for gun purchasers.

1994   Congress passes the Violent Crime Control and Law Enforcement Act, which includes the Federal Assault Weapons Ban.

1995   The U.S. Supreme Court strikes down the Gun-Free School Zones Act. Congress revises the law and passes a new Gun-Free School Zones Act.

1998   The FBI unveils the National Instant Criminal Background Check System, which allows gun dealers to perform instant background checks.

1999   Two students bring four guns and many homemade explosives to Columbine High School in Colorado, where they carry out a massacre that kills thirteen innocent people. This incident sparks a wave of gun-control debate.

2004   The Federal Assault Weapons Ban expires. Congress declines to renew it.

2005   David Hernandez Arroyo Sr. goes on a shooting rampage in Tyler, Texas, killing himself and two other people. Congress passes the Protection of Lawful Commerce in Arms Act. The law shields gun manufacturers and dealers from certain civil lawsuits related to gun violence.

2007   Cho Seung Hui opens fire at Virginia Tech University, killing thirty-two people.

2008   In *District of Columbia v. Heller*, the U.S. Supreme Court rules that the Second Amendment guarantees individual gun rights. Football pro Plaxico Burress makes headlines by accidentally shooting himself in the leg with an illegally concealed handgun.

2009   Richard Poplawski kills three police officers during a four-hour shootout in Pittsburgh, Pennsylvania.
Members of the U.S. Congress propose two laws to more
tightly regulate gun shows.

2010   A congressional committee discusses restricting the
Second Amendment rights of suspected terrorists.

2011   Jared Lee Loughner opens fire at a supermarket in Casas
Adobes, Arizona. He kills six people and wounds thirteen
others, including U.S. representative Gabrielle Giffords.
The shootings spark renewed debate, with President
Obama calling for stricter enforcement of commonsense
gun control.

GLOSSARY

amendment: a change or an addition

assault weapons: automatic or semiautomatic weapons designed for military-style attacks

automatic weapon: a weapon that fires multiple rounds of ammunition with a single trigger pull

cache: a hidden supply

caliber: the diameter of a gun barrel or of ammunition

castle law: a law that gives people the right to use lethal force to defend themselves from intruders in their homes

colony: a dependent territory

conservatives: people who support established institutions and cultural norms and who generally favor a limited role for government. In political spheres, conservatives are often called the Right.

crossbow: a mechanized bow that fires short, heavy, pointed projectiles called bolts

deter: to prevent

felony: a serious crime

fugitive: a person on the run from law enforcement

handgun: a small handheld gun, such as a pistol

liability: legal penalties

liberals: people who support the idea that institutions and cultural norms can change as societal attitudes shift and who generally support a broad role for government. In political spheres, liberals are often called the Left.

lobbying: trying to influence public officials

magazine: a clip that contains ammunition and feeds it into a weapon

mandated: required

microstamping: the practice of laser-engraving a design on a gun's firing pin. This design leaves a unique mark on the casing of fired ammunition. Microstamping is also called ballistic imprinting or ballistic engraving.

militia: a small, local, loosely organized military group of citizens rather than trained professionals

misdemeanor: a lesser crime

precedent: a social or legal model

rifle: a long gun with spiraling grooves engraved inside its barrel

semiautomatic weapon: a weapon with automatic and quick loading of ammunition ready to fire after each pull of the trigger

shotgun: a long gun whose barrel is smooth inside

straw purchase: a transaction in which one person buys a firearm on another person's behalf

terrorist: someone who uses violence to create fear, usually to promote a movement or a cause

tommy gun: a lightweight machine gun

tyranny: cruel and oppressive government

SOURCE NOTES

9 Michael A. Bellesiles, *Arming America: The Origins of a National Gun Culture* (New York: Alfred A. Knopf, 2000), 18.

14 Ibid., 76.

17 Ibid., 210.

17 Thomas Jefferson, "Thomas Jefferson to William Smith: November 13, 1787," Library of Congress, July 22, 2010, http://www.loc.gov/exhibits/jefferson/105.html (January 6, 2011).

18 Joint Committee on Printing, "The Constitution of the United States with Index and the Declaration of Independence," GPO, July 25, 2007, http://frwebgate.access.gpo.gov/cgi-bin/getdoc.cgi?dbname=110_cong_documents&docid=f:hd051.110.pdf (November 18, 2010).

18 Don Higginbotham, *Revolution in America: Considerations and Comparisons* (Charlottesville: University of Virginia Press, 2005), 105.

19 Brian Doherty, *Gun Control on Trial: Inside the Supreme Court Battle over the Second Amendment* (Washington, DC: Cato Institute, 2008), 8–9.

34 Supreme Court of the United States, "Syllabus: District of Columbia et al. v. Heller," Cornell University Law School Legal Information Institute: Supreme Court Collection, June 26, 2008, http://www.law.cornell.edu/supct/html/07-290.ZS.html (November 22, 2010).

35 Nick Allen, "Gabrielle Giffords Shooting: US Gun Law Likely to Be Unaffected," *The Telegraph*, January 9, 2011, http://www.telegraph.co.uk/news/worldnews/us-politics/8249300/Gabrielle-Giffords-shooting-US-gun-law-likely-to-be-unaffected.html (April 1, 2011).

35 Barack Obama, "President Obama: We Must Seek Agreement on Gun Reforms," *Arizona Daily Star*, March 13, 2011, http://azstarnet.com/news/opinion/mailbag/article_011e7118-8951-5206-a878-39bfbc9dc89d.html (April 1, 2011).

41 Reuters, "School Shootings Reignite Gun Control Debate," MSNBC, October 23, 2006, http://www.msnbc.msn.com/id/15386044 (November 30, 2010).

42–43 Chris Hawley, "Mexico Says Gun Controls Undermined by U.S. Laws," *USA Today*, April 1, 2009, A5.

46 Karin Kiewra, "Guns and Suicide: A Fatal Link," *Harvard Public Health Review*, n.d., http://www.hsph.harvard.edu/news/hphr/social-health-hazards/guns-and-suicide/index.html (November 29, 2010).

48 MacNeil/Lehrer Productions, "Gun Control Debate Revisited on Anniversary of Virginia Tech Shooting," PBS *NewsHour,* April 16, 2009,

http://www.pbs.org/newshour/bb/law/jan-june09/gunlaws_04-16.html
(November 30, 2010).

57–58   Dana Milbank, "Terrorists Who Want to Buy Guns Have Friends on Capitol
        Hill," *Washington Post*, May 6, 2010, http://www.washingtonpost.com/
        wp-dyn/content/article/2010/05/05/AR2010050505211.html (December 1,
        2010).

58   Ibid.

58   Huma Khan and Z. Byron Wolf, "Guns and Terror: Should People on U.S.
        Watch List Be Barred from Buying Firearms?" ABC News, May 5, 2010,
        http://abcnews.go.com/Politics/individuals-terror-watch-list-allowed-buy-
        guns-90/story?id=10561483 (December 1, 2010).

59   MacNeil/Lehrer Productions, "Gun Control Debate Revisited."

60–61   Antonin Scalia, "Opinion of the Court: District of Columbia v. Heller,"
        Cornell University Law School Legal Information Institute: Supreme Court
        Collection, June 26, 2008, http://www.law.cornell.edu/supct/html/07-290
        .ZO.html (December 1, 2010).

65   Harry Browne, "For Safety Sake, Repeal All the Gun Laws," *Ethical
        Spectacle*, June 2000, http://www.spectacle.org/0600/browne.html
        (December 2, 2010).

73   Liz Robbins and Sean D. Hamill, "Gunman Kills 3 Police Officers in
        Pittsburgh," *New York Times*, April 4, 2009, http://www.nytimes
        .com/2009/04/05/us/05pittsburgh.html (December 2, 2010).

73   Ibid.

74   James McReynolds, "Opinion of the Court: United States v. Miller,"
        Cornell University Law School Legal Information Institute: Supreme
        Court Collection, May 15, 1939, http://www.law.cornell.edu/supct/html/
        historics/USSC_CR_0307_0174_ZO.html (December 3, 2010).

77   MacNeil/Lehrer Productions, "Ban Gunned Down?" PBS *NewsHour*, March
        22, 1996, http://www.pbs.org/newshour/bb/congress/gun_ban_3-22.html
        (December 6, 2010).

78   CBS Interactive, "Heated Debate over Assault Weapons," CBS *Face the
        Nation*, April 19, 2009, http://www.cbsnews.com/stories/2009/04/19/ftn/
        main4954990.shtml (December 6, 2010).

85   Tom Scheck, "Loophole or Individual Right?" *MPRnews*, February 19, 2009,
        http://minnesota.publicradio.org/collections/special/columns/polinaut/
        archive/2009/02/loophole_or_ind.shtml (December 6, 2010).

85   Ibid.

86   Mike Kaszuba, "Gun Show Ban Draws Debate but No Vote," *StarTribune*, March 5, 2010, http://www.startribune.com/politics/state/86627222.html (December 6, 2010).

86   Scheck, "Loophole or Individual Right?"

86   Ibid.

92   Mike Cook, "Closing a Weapons Loophole," Minnesota House of Representatives Public Information Services, March 11, 2010, http://www .house.leg.state.mn.us/sessionweekly/art.asp?ls_year=86&issueid_ =52&storyid=1644&year_=2010 (December 7, 2010).

93   Dan Olson, "Felons Slip through Gun Background Checks," *Minnesota Public Radio*, January 16, 2002, http://news.minnesota.publicradio.org/ features/200201/16_olsond_gunsales/ (December 7, 2010).

102   William M. Welch, "Critics Take Aim at Gun Buybacks," *USA Today*, March 18, 2008, http://www.usatoday.com/news/nation/2008-03-17-gun- buybacks_N.htm (December 7, 2010).

103   Ibid.

SELECTED BIBLIOGRAPHY

Bellesiles, Michael A. *Arming America: The Origins of a National Gun Culture.* New York: Alfred A Knopf, 2000.

Carter, Gregg Lee. *Gun Control in the United States: A Reference Handbook.* Santa Barbara, CA: ABC-CLIO, 2006.

Doherty, Brian. *Gun Control on Trial: Inside the Supreme Court Battle over the Second Amendment.* Washington, DC: Cato Institute, 2008.

Gottlieb, Alan M., and Dave Workman. *Assault on Weapons: The Campaign to Eliminate Your Guns.* Bellevue, WA: Merril Press, 2009.

Higginbotham, Don. *Revolution in America: Considerations and Comparisons.* Charlottesville: University of Virginia Press, 2005.

LaPierre, Wayne. *Guns, Freedom, and Terrorism.* Nashville: Thomas Nelson, 2003.

Lott, John R. *More Guns Less Crime: Understanding Crime and Gun Control Laws.* Chicago: University of Chicago Press, 2010.

Patrick, John J. *The Bill of Rights: A History in Documents.* New York: Oxford University Press, 2003.

Reynolds, Jack. *A People Armed and Free: The Truth about the Second Amendment.* Bloomington, IN: 1st Books, 2003.

Roleff, Tamara L. *Gun Control.* Farmington Hills, MI: Thomson Gale, 2007.

Wilson, Harry L. *Guns, Gun Control, and Elections: The Politics and Policy of Firearms.* Lanham, MD: Rowman and Littlefield, 2007.

ORGANIZATIONS TO CONTACT

Brady Campaign to Prevent Gun Violence
> The Brady Center to Prevent Gun Violence
> 1225 Eye Street NW, Suite 1100
> Washington, DC 20005
> 202-898-0792
> http://www.bradycampaign.org
> The Brady Campaign to Prevent Gun Violence is a major political force
> in pursuit of stricter gun-control laws.

Bureau of Alcohol, Tobacco, Firearms and Explosives (ATF)
> Office of Public and Governmental Affairs
> 99 New York Avenue NE, Room 5S 144
> Washington, DC 20226
> 800-800-3855
> http://www.atf.gov
> The ATF is a federal government agency. It is responsible for protecting
> the United States against the illegal use and trafficking of firearms, the
> illegal use and storage of explosives, acts of arson and bombings, acts
> of terrorism, and the illegal diversion of alcohol and tobacco products.

Coalition to Stop Gun Violence (CSGV)
> 1424 L Street NW, Suite 2-1
> Washington, DC 20005
> 202-408-0061
> http://www.csgv.org
> The Coalition to Stop Gun Violence works to reduce gun violence in the
> United States through education, research, and political advocacy.

Gun Owners of America (GOA)
> 8001 Forbes Place, Suite 102
> Springfield, VA 22151
> 703-321-8585
> http://gunowners.org
> GOA is a nonprofit lobbying organization formed to preserve and
> defend the Second Amendment rights of gun owners.

National Rifle Association of America (NRA)
11250 Waples Mill Road
Fairfax, VA 22030
800-672-3888
http://nra.org
The NRA supports gun owners with information about firearms, magazine articles, political advocacy, and much more.

Second Amendment Foundation (SAF)
12500 NE 10th Place
Bellevue, WA 98005
425-454-7012
http://www.saf.org
The Second Amendment Foundation is a gun-rights organization dedicated to promoting understanding of the Second Amendment.

Violence Policy Center
1730 Rhode Island Avenue NW, Suite 1014
Washington, DC 20036
202-822-8200
http://www.vpc.org
The Violence Policy Center works to reduce gun violence through research, political advocacy, and education.

FURTHER INFORMATION

BOOKS

Fisanick, Christina. *Gun Control*. Detroit: Greenhaven, 2010.
Read more about the gun-control debate around the world in this book in the Global Viewpoints series.

Gold, Susan Dudley. *Gun Control*. Tarrytown, NY: Marshall Cavendish, 2004.
This book tracks the history of gun control from the writing of the Second Amendment to the modern debate over school shootings.

Gonzales, Doreen. *A Look at the Second Amendment: To Keep and Bear Arms*. Berkeley Heights, NJ: Enslow Publishers, 2008.
The author takes an in-depth look at the Second Amendment, investigating why it exists, how it has been interpreted, and what it means.

Graham, Amy. *A Look at the Bill of Rights: Protecting the Rights of Americans*. Berkeley Heights, NJ: Enslow, 2008.
Learn more about the Bill of Rights, how it came to be, and the rights it guarantees all Americans.

How Goverment Works series. Minneapolis: Lerner Publications Company, 2004.
This series on the United States government includes a title on the Bill of Rights and the Constitution.

Hubbard-Brown, Janet. *How the Constitution Was Created*. New York: Chelsea House, 2007.
Read about the framing of the Constitution, the approval of the Bill of Rights, and what the Constitution means to Americans.

Kiesbye, Stefan. *Gun Violence*. Detroit: Greenhaven, 2008.
This collection of essays presents various viewpoints on the debate over gun rights and gun control.

Lunger, Norman L. *Big Bang: The Loud Debate over Gun Control*. Minneapolis: Twenty-First Century Books, 2002.
The author delves into many aspects of the gun-control debate, examining the pros and cons of gun control.

Ransom, Candace. *Who Wrote the U.S. Constitution?* Minneapolis: Lerner
Publications Company, 2011.
Discover the facts about the 1787 Convention and the writing of the
Constitution.

Streissguth, Tom. *District of Columbia v. Heller: The Right to Bear Arms Case.*
Berkeley Heights, NJ: Enslow Publishers, 2010.
Discover the details of the landmark Supreme Court case that found
the right to bear arms is an individual right of all Americans.

FILM

Bowling for Columbine. DVD. Los Angeles: MGM, 2003.
In this Academy Award–winning documentary, activist filmmaker
Michael Moore explores his view of the reasons behind the United
States' high rate of gun violence.

WEBSITES

American Firearms Institute
http://www.americanfirearms.org
The American Firearms Institute is a pro-gun organization that fights
for gun rights in the United States. The website includes fact sheets,
statistics, and information on federal and state gun laws.

Bill of Rights
http://www.archives.gov/exhibits/charters/bill_of_rights.html
Read the entire Bill of Rights, and see a photograph of the original
document. Also, learn about other changes made to the Constitution.

Common Sense about Kids and Guns
http://www.kidsandguns.org
This website is sponsored by a nonprofit coalition of gun-control
advocates, gun makers and others in the firearms industry, child safety
advocates, child welfare advocates, crime prevention advocates, and
mayors committed to working together to protect U.S. children from
gun deaths and injuries. Here you can read about the impact guns can
have on kids and teens and find safety tips for both children and parents.

GunCite

http://www.guncite.com
This gun-rights website contains many links to essays, articles, statistics, and opinions about gun control.

National Rifle Association Institute for Legislative Action (NRA-ILA)

http://www.nraila.org
The NRA-ILA is the lobbying arm of the National Rifle Association. Its mission is to preserve the gun rights of all Americans. Its website includes information on gun laws being proposed or debated and gives overviews of state and federal gun laws.

New York Times

http://www.nytimes.com
The online version of the *New York Times* keeps readers up to date with news from around the world. It is an excellent source for discovering the latest news about gun violence and gun policy.

PAX: The Center to Prevent Youth Violence

http://paxusa.org
PAX is an organization working to end the crisis of youth violence in the United States. PAX develops public health and safety campaigns that promote the simple steps parents, kids, teachers, and others can take to prevent youth violence.

INDEX

PHOTO ACKNOWLEDGMENTS

The images in this book are used with the permission of: © James Palka/Getty Images, pp. 4–5; © Andrea Rescigno/Alamy, pp. 8–9; The Art Archive/Musée du Louvre Paris/Alfredo Dagli Orti, p. 10; © Hulton Archive/Getty Images, p. 11; The Art Archive/Gunshots, p. 12; The Art Archive/Culver Pictures, p. 13; Library of Congress, p. 15 (LC-USZ62-19); © Stock Montage/Archive Photos/Getty Images, p. 17; © MPI/Archive Photos/Getty Images, p. 20; © Mary Evans Picture Library/The Image Works, p. 21; © Chicago History Museum/Archive Photos/Getty Images, p. 22; © Francis Miller/Time & Life Pictures/Getty Images, p. 25; © Donald Uhrbrock/Time & Life Pictures/Getty Images, p. 26; AP Photo, p. 27 (left); AP Photo/Charles Kelly, p. 27 (right); © Tim Sloan/AFP/Getty Images, p. 28; AP Photo/Ron Edmonds, p. 30; AP Photo/Doug Mills, p. 31; © Mark Leffingwell/Getty Images, p. 32; © Robert Hanashiro/USA TODAY, p. 33; AP Photo/Tyler Morning Telegraph, Herb Nygren Jr., pp. 38–39; © Chris Hawley/USA TODAY, pp. 42, 43; © Bill Pugliano/Getty Images, p. 44; AP Photo/Bill Haber, p. 45; © Ricky Carioti/The Washington Post/Getty Images, p. 47; AP Photo/John Carrington, Pool, p. 53; © Stan Honda/AFP/Getty Images, pp. 54–55; © Chris Hondros/Getty Images, p. 57; © Mark Wilson/Getty Images, p. 60; © Jeff Swinger/USA TODAY, p. 62; © Jupiterimages/Comstock Images/Getty Images, p. 63; AP Photo/Gene J. Puskar, pp. 70–71; AP Photo/Misha Japaridze, p. 72; © Luis Acosta/AFP/Getty Images, p. 75; © Tim Dillon/USA TODAY, p. 79; © Ethan Miller/Getty Images, pp. 82, 97; Photo courtesy Andrew VonBank, MN House of Representatives, pp. 84–85; AP Photo/Elise Amendola, p. 87; © Peter Hvizdak/The Image Works, p. 88; AP Photo/Mark J. Terrill, p. 95; © Robert Deutsch/USA TODAY, p. 98; © Laura Westlund/Independent Picture Service, p. 99; AP Photo/Matt York, p. 100; © Robyn Beck/AFP/Getty Images, p. 102; © H. Darr Beiser/USA TODAY, pp. 104–105; AP Photo/Seth Perlman, p. 106.

Front cover: © Scott Sroka/National Geographic/Getty Images.

Main body text set in USA TODAY Roman Regular 10.5/15.

ABOUT THE AUTHOR

Matt Doeden is a freelance author and editor living in Minnesota. He has written and edited hundreds of children's books on topics ranging from genetic engineering to rock climbing to monster trucks.